Signal 8

An Australian
Paramedic's Story

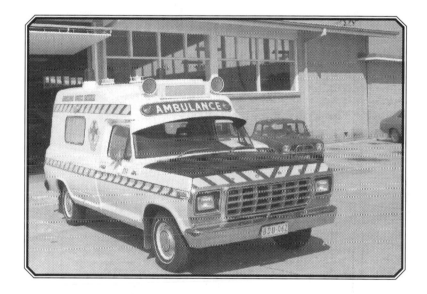

ERIK SCHANSSEMA

BALBOA.
PRESS
A DIVISION OF HAY HOUSE

Balboa Press books may be ordered through booksellers or by contacting:

Balboa Press
A Division of Hay House
1663 Liberty Drive
Bloomington, IN 47403
www.balboapress.com.au
1 (877) 407-4847

Because of the dynamic nature of the Internet, any web addresses or links contained in this book may have changed since publication and may no longer be valid. The views expressed in this work are solely those of the author and do not necessarily reflect the views of the publisher, and the publisher hereby disclaims any responsibility for them.

The author of this book does not dispense medical advice or prescribe the use of any technique as a form of treatment for physical, emotional, or medical problems without the advice of a physician, either directly or indirectly. The intent of the author is only to offer information of a general nature to help you in your quest for emotional and spiritual well-being. In the event you use any of the information in this book for yourself, which is your constitutional right, the author and the publisher assume no responsibility for your actions.

Any people depicted in stock imagery provided by Thinkstock are models, and such images are being used for illustrative purposes only. Certain stock imagery © Thinkstock.

Print information available on the last page.

ISBN: 978-1-5043-0600-3 (sc)

Balboa Press rev. date: 01/17/2017

Dedication

This book is dedicated to the love of my life—my wife, best friend, and eternal soul partner, Belen, who passed away suddenly in October 2014. Belen loved and supported me throughout our life together, including my thirty-six-year ambulance service career. She endured our times apart due to shift work and tolerated my post-nightshift crabbiness. Belen was my advocate and saviour when in 1986 I suffered an unanticipated decompensation crisis (nervous breakdown). She successfully argued against a proposal to treat me with electro convulsive therapy (ECR) and challenged my medication regime, which she believed was exacerbating my illness.

To what degree my paramedic experiences contributed to my becoming ill I cannot say; readers may draw their own conclusions.

This book is also dedicated to the wellbeing of all past, present, and future paramedics, medical and nursing staff, emergency service workers, and volunteers.

Belen enjoying the view from Edinburgh castle

For Shirley, Julian, Darcy, Patrick, and Zoe

Contents

Foreword

Every ambulance officer or paramedic has a story to tell. Erik's story reminded me of the history of the ambulance service and the people we both worked with, but most of all, it has highlighted the nature of ambulance work and how it can be compared to entering a war zone (albeit without the constant feeling that your life is at risk).

If it were possible to travel back to Frankston Branch in 1977, when Erik started work with Peninsula Ambulance Service, you would hear discussions about difficult or interesting cases and at times, some funny stories. What you wouldn't hear was anyone speaking about the stresses involved in being a paramedic and how the accumulation of traumatic incidents can affect a person over time. To this day, you will hear paramedics speak about "good jobs." These are the ones that are interesting, that are challenging, or that make you feel you have made a difference or learnt something. The culture doesn't allow for anyone to admit to being stressed, and to do so is viewed as a weakness and career suicide.

It was the Russell Street bombing (Victoria Police headquarters) just prior to Easter in 1986 that led to the establishment of the Victorian Ambulance Crisis Counselling Unit (VACCU) and confidential counselling for all ambulance employees and their immediate family. Erik's generation of paramedics, after nine years of service, was now able to access six counselling sessions per year, but unfortunately, the stigma of seeking help prevented the majority from using these services.

Having worked with Erik for several years, I would describe him as someone I would trust to treat my own family members, which, as paramedics know, is the highest compliment you can make to another paramedic. I was surprised to read about Erik's admission to the Melbourne Clinic for an acute decompensation crisis and his diagnosis of OCD, as I had no idea that he suffered from these illnesses. I wasn't surprised, however, that he felt the need to keep these issues a secret, as the stigma is such that no one would be prepared to risk disclosing this information, even to close friends.

For most paramedics, their spouse is a major support person in helping them deal with the stresses of the job, and this is especially true of Belen. She was always a very warm and friendly person who was pleased to see you and have a chat. She was a person who cared for other people and clearly applied her skills in supporting Erik in his job as a MICA Team Manager. Her death was a big loss to Erik and his family.

In his author's note, Erik has shown concern for the welfare of his past colleagues. This concern is justified, as there are many paramedics who, after some months or years of retirement, realise that what they thought was fatigue from working too hard was actually undiagnosed depression, anxiety, or stress. My message for you is that it is never too late to speak to someone, and a good place to start is with your local doctor, who can refer you to a professional counsellor for assessment and treatment.

For people contemplating a career as a paramedic, be aware that we take on this career with the belief that the advantages of personal growth and the satisfaction we get from helping others far outweigh the disadvantages, but it is to our own detriment if we ignore the disadvantages. Be prepared to take the advice of the people who have gone before you, and take a proactive approach to caring for yourself instead of trying to pretend that stress doesn't exist.

Knowing the attitude that many people have towards mental illness, I felt compelled to point out the fact that following Erik's diagnosis and hospital admission, he was still able to have a successful MICA paramedic career that spanned another fourteen years. I ponder the question of "Would he have been successful in his MICA Team Manager application if his illness was common knowledge at that time?"

My concern regarding our attitudes towards and the stigma surrounding mental illness is that it prevents our paramedics from being proactive about caring for their mental health. We are probably several years away from the average paramedic being prepared to openly disclose a mental health issue, but I think we are currently on the verge of having the average paramedic agree that caring for our mental health is important and that we should all be improving our education in this area, developing a mental health plan and making use of our six free appointments per year with one of our VACCU psychologists.

I have no doubt that many of our current and retired paramedics will reflect on their ambulance paramedic career as they are reading this book. Hopefully, it will bring back more pleasant than bad memories, but if for whatever reason you feel the need to speak with someone, I would encourage you to speak with your own general practitioner, who can refer you to a suitable professional in your area. I am also happy for you to contact our Ambulance Victoria Peer Support Program, or one of the other organisations as follows.

Ambulance Victoria Peer Support

Phone: 1-800 626 377 (1800 MANERS), (Press 1 and leave your name and contact number)

Email: peer.support@ambulance.vic.gov.au   i

Lifeline: 131114

Beyondblue: 1 300 22 4636

Hopefully, the future for paramedics will be a proactive approach to preincident stress awareness education, stress management plans, stress management training for managers, and a culture where it is considered normal to speak to a professional counsellor after we have attended a run of distressing or "bad jobs." It is only by doing the above that we will identify mental health issues early and prevent some of the bad outcomes that our forebears have experienced.

By sharing his story with us all, Erik has contributed to the solution. As paramedics share their stories, it helps to reduce the stigma around and to educate others on the issues experienced by paramedics and other emergency service workers. I wish Erik and his family all the best for the future and thank him for putting his story into words for us all to read.

David Cooper

Peer Support Co-ordinator—Ambulance Victoria

April 2016

Author's Note

It is only in recent years that the mental and physical injuries associated with emergency ambulance work have been recognised in the broader community, including finally some politicians. This book describes my pre-ambulance occupations and how these unsatisfying experiences led me to seek more meaningful and valuable work. I describe my introduction to the ambulance service and my progression from student ambulance officer (AO) to Mobile Intensive Care Ambulance (MICA) paramedic and Team Manager over my operational career, spanning the period from 1977 to 2001.

I also describe how, nine years into my ambulance career, I became suddenly ill. I was diagnosed with an acute decompensation crisis (a description of the illness previously known as nervous breakdown) and obsessive compulsive disorder (OCD). My operational career effectively ended on New Year's Eve 1999, when I sustained serious work-related injuries. Prior to this occurring, I had been aware of a deep physical and psychological fatigue that I feared could lead to a recurrence of my 1986 illness. Because of this, I found myself unexpectedly relieved when my orthopaedic surgeon advised me that my injuries meant that I could never return to operational ambulance duties. Despite this and my now uncertain future, I felt I still had much to contribute to Metropolitan Ambulance Service (MAS); consequently, for a time I worked in paramedic education whilst concurrently managing my MICA Team.

During this period, an opportunity arose to assist MAS in its efforts to seek accreditation in the internationally recognised quality and safety standards, ISO 9001:2000 and AS4801:2001. This was achieved by MAS in 2001 and has been maintained to this day. My work, guided by my mentor Les Taylor (MAS' business manager at the time), was recognised by the service resulting in the establishment of the new position of operations service improvement co-ordinator. I applied for and was appointed to this position, requiring though that I relinquish my team manager position and effectively formally ending my operational career. My new position led to my writing many of the service's operational and nonoperational policies, procedures and work instructions, including compiling the MAS Infection Control manual. I later qualified as an internal auditor of both ISO 9001:2000 and AS4801:2001 and conducted many wide-ranging internal audits aimed at ensuring MAS retained both standards. My audit reports included proposals for improvement in many areas of the service's activities, many of which were subsequently adopted.

During my ambulance career and beyond, a number of colleagues became affected by, and at times incapacitated by, mental illness or serious injury. In the case of mental illness, it is difficult to reconcile how prolonged exposure to human tragedy and trauma may affect an individual. Contributing factors such as an individual's character, life experiences, and personal circumstances play their part. Tragically, too many colleagues and friends arrived at the awful decision that they could not go on and ended their lives, sometimes with no immediate warning signs to family or colleagues.

The psychological effects and physical injuries associated with operational ambulance work cannot be completely eliminated and will continue to cause pain and suffering to paramedics and consequently to their partners, families, and friends. In the earlier days of my career, ambulance officers suffering from mental health issues had no access to formal assistance. Looking back, many were suffering from what is today described as post-traumatic stress disorder (PTSD). The situation for today's paramedics has improved significantly, beginning with the establishment of the Ambulance Victoria (AV) Peer Support Program and its associated services. The recent announcement that AV will work directly with the Victorian Beyondblue organisation to provide psychological training for all paramedics is encouraging and bodes well for the future.

During my early operational years, all AOs were male and thus tended to suffer in silence, often turning to alcohol and tobacco as a means of dealing with the traumatic side of ambulance work. I cannot recall any conversations from those times where we discussed our feelings regarding our attendances at traumatic cases, no matter how severe or disturbing. Instead, we protected ourselves behind a screen of black humour, peculiar to ambulance staff. For example, we often arrived at a case to find a deceased patient's body to be in a state of rigor mortis. During these days, and depending on the circumstances of a patient's demise, we were required to transport the body to a public hospital mortuary. A patient who had deceased whilst seated and in rigor mortis would remain with limbs locked in the position when death had occurred. We were then required to lift the body onto our stretcher and cover it with a sheet or blanket, hoping not to share the disturbing scene with hapless passers-by as we loaded the stretcher into our ambulance. Such situations could have an element of macabre humour, kept between us and never reflecting any callousness or disrespect on our part.

My description of some of the aspects of ambulance training in the late 1970s may give an impression of *Dad's Army* types of scenarios. This is unintentional and misleading, as the training we received, combined with our evolving clinical knowledge and improving skills, set us up well to provide quality and professional care to our patients, albeit within the limits of our treatment protocols, drugs, and equipment of the time. We learned to thoroughly assess our patients and evaluate their signs and symptoms associated with the myriad diseases or injuries we encountered. At the same time, we were often reminded by our trainers never to declare a patient's diagnosis but only to provide a patient's provisional assessment. Nevertheless, our assessments were usually accurate and reflected the patient's final diagnosis. To aid in our learning, most of us would follow up on our patient's progress on our subsequent visits to the hospital.

With this book, my intention is not to provide a chronological or complete history of ambulance training, as it was at the time, nor of my operational experiences. Rather, I describe a few of the cases I attended in an effort to provide an insight into how it feels to be confronted by human tragedy and how we must set aside our normal reactions to revolting situations and focus our attention on providing optimum patient care. Repeated exposure to such events sooner or later extracts a toll on the individual paramedic, at times also adversely impacting personal relationships with partners, family, and friends.

All ambulance paramedics begin their careers hoping and desiring to save lives and otherwise improve patient outcomes, although what this might entail and its personal costs are yet beyond their experience. Prehospital care provided by paramedics frequently results in improved patient outcomes, including reduction in the length of hospital stays. However, as in all aspects of medical care, errors may occur, or they may be imagined. Of course, any actions (or inactions) resulting in adverse patient outcomes are unintentional. For paramedics, the thought that their actions or inactions may have caused patient harm can be deeply disturbing, often resulting in a lack of confidence and belief in their patient-care skills. Such a perceived or actual error overshadows the many cases where the paramedic has effectively saved patients' lives or contributed significantly to their improved outcomes.

I hope that sharing some of my experiences may assist current and future paramedics by understanding they are not isolated and that others have trodden the path before them. The cases I relate in this book are not in any way intended to sensationalise the events nor are they aimed at deliberately upsetting readers. I chose these incidents as they were the first that came to mind when I was considering examples of various case types. Given that they were the first to come to mind, I am left supposing that I remain marked by them. I also hope to convey the physical and mental strain that accompanies paramedics when presented with the challenges of making the right and appropriate patient-care decisions, increased exponentially in multiple patient incidents.

Your survival, physical and psychological, is as vital as that of any patient to whom you may attend. Now, looking in from the outside, I thank you for choosing to become paramedics; you have much to be proud of.

I apologise to past colleagues whose names I can no longer associate with specific cases. I also point out that where I have described clinical conditions, I have done so bearing in mind that readers may not have a medical background.

I would like to thank all my past operational and nonoperational colleagues who shared my ambulance career; all of you were, and are, dedicated to improving both patient care and Ambulance Victoria in general. I also extend my thanks to all hospital and emergency service staff with whom we shared tragedies but also good humour and understanding.

I thank my brother, Aafko, who encouraged me during the writing of this book and contributed significantly through his constructive comments, suggestions, and corrections. I thank also David Cooper, my ex-MICA colleague, for writing his thoughtful Foreword to this work. As crewmembers, David and I attended several of the cases described. David has been and remains a key driving force behind the establishment of the AV Peer Support Program and its related services. In recognition of his substantial contribution and dedication, David was nominated for Australian of the Year in 2016.

For the sake of privacy, I have not identified patient names or specific case locations, and I apologise to ex-colleagues whose names I can no longer associate directly with some of the cases described.

1

Stepping Out

A Teenage Banker and Gunslinger

Like many young men unsure of who they are, let alone what they want to be and do in life, I decided to leave high school when I was sixteen. I lived in Geelong, and at the end of the 1968 school year, I had not yet completed Year 12. Although I knew I was capable of progressing through to university, I had not enjoyed the later years of high school and believed I could assist my parents by saving them the burden of any costs associated with my further education. Still, I had no clear idea of a career path, possessing only a vague dream of training as a Royal Australian Air Force (RAAF) pilot. However, as I had not completed Year 12, or matriculation, as it was then known, this was beyond my reach.

Fortunately, jobs for school leavers were relatively easy to come by in the late 1960s, and with no great purpose in mind, I made an appointment with the manager of the Commercial Bank of Australia (CBA) at the main Geelong city branch. It turned out to be a short interview but included a very peculiar question. He asked, "Do you row?" I had to admit that, no, I didn't. Apparently, he was looking to recruit new members for the bank's rowing team. Fortunately, he was not dissuaded by my lack of rowing skills, and he employed me on a full-time basis, beginning immediately.

I was still only sixteen when I began my banking career. My first task was learning how to accurately count the various denominational banknotes (Australia had only converted to decimal currency in 1966) by using a rubber thimble on my index finger, moistened as required on a wet sponge placed in a small bowl. My first impression of the banking industry was one of an atmosphere of reserve and seriousness, as reflected by senior staff outfitted in dark suits and mandatory white shirts. I soon found, though, that banking staff was not devoid of humour, as demonstrated when tricks were played on new employees. My favourite was sending a new employee to a rival bank branch to ask to borrow their scales to "balance the books." I'm pleased to report that I didn't fall for that one.

Banks in Geelong at the time had a shared arrangement, whereby if one was low on coins or particular banknote denominations, the other would assist. I was introduced to this arrangement one day when I was handed a loaded .38-calibre pistol and instructed to conceal it in my jacket pocket. Still only sixteen and naive, I assumed that this was usual bank procedure. I kept my fingers well away from the trigger. I was directed to walk some distance behind two senior bank tellers as they made their way to the nearby CBA branch. Arriving there safely, the CBA banknotes were counted and exchanged for bags of coins. The tellers then made their way back, lugging a heavy white calico bag in each hand. I had not been provided with any instructions regarding the operation of the weapon, certainly not what to do in the unlikely event of a hold-up.

Within a few months, I was transferred to the tiny CBA branch at North Geelong, located directly next door to a Bank of New South Wales branch. As armed bank robberies were relatively common in Victoria at the time, the two respective bank managers had concocted a scheme; each would come to the assistance of the other during a hold-up. Consequently, identical alarms were installed in both buildings, the concept being that when held up, the affected bank teller would silently trip a metal bar by lifting his toe under his teller's desk, setting off the alarm in the neighbouring branch. Following this, the plan was for staff of the unaffected bank to rush in with loaded weapons and apprehend the bank robber/s. The alarms, however, were so sensitive to touch that a teller might not be aware that he (all tellers were male at the time) had tripped it. This led to the alarming sight of our neighbours appearing at our bank with weapons drawn. Happily, no hold-ups occurred during my time there.

The CBA's North Geelong branch was in its entirety not much larger than an average domestic bedroom. It included a partitioned manager's office, a single teller's station, and an administrative area combined with a kitchenette. The manager was very much an old-school banker, close to retirement age, gruff, and difficult to communicate with. He was in the habit of paying hopeful visits to the homes of lottery winners, encouraging them to open new CBA bank accounts. Privacy didn't seem to factor in those days, as he seemed to have no difficulty in identifying winners and their addresses.

Almost all bank administrative tasks at the time were completed by hand. Those involving customer accounts fell to me, the junior. I operated the single piece of technology available, a typewriter-like mechanical device into which account sheets were inserted and updated. All related calculations were completed without the aid of a calculator. I worked out of public sight, a screen separating me from the teller's location. Behind me was a small sink with tea-making facilities. Each day, without fail, the manager emerged from his office to make himself a pot of tea. He timed his appearance to coincide with my or the teller's lunch break and stood over the sink loudly bringing up phlegm from deep in his barrel chest and expectorating into our communal sink. A very foul man indeed.

As the branch junior, the manager expected that I perform any menial branch tasks, extending to washing his private vehicle. One hot summer day, he directed me to scrub the vinyl-clad seats of his pride, a Holden Kingswood (a popular Australian sedan), using only a toothbrush. Only seventeen and working in an environment where bank managers were seen as omnipotent, I felt I had no choice but to comply with whatever nonbanking task he set for me. I recall seeing a staff report, which I was not entitled to see, where he described me as an "arty type." To this day, I don't know how he arrived at his assessment.

The Reluctant Traveller

As was the norm at the time, I was soon placed on the general CBA relieving staff roster, meaning that I would temporarily fill the position of a staff member who was on leave or ill. The roster covered all Victorian branches, and it was the responsibility of the reserve staff member to make arrangements to travel wherever the bank demanded. The belief at the time was that to be considered for promotion, time on the reserve roster was a necessary evil. Bank wages, particularly for juniors, were poor, and I couldn't afford to purchase a car. Instead, I had seen *Easy Rider,* the cult movie of the time, which inspired me to purchase a 100cc Honda motorbike.

I spent many months on the relieving staff roster, including a stint at an outer-eastern Melbourne branch, where one of the tellers had allegedly been transferring multiple small amounts from customer accounts into his own account. Finally, suspicions arose, and accusing fingers were pointed in his direction when he arrived for work in a new car. I'm unaware of his fate, but we were left to work late after each business day to try to locate each fraudulent entry. Many weeks passed before the branch could declare that its books were finally balanced.

From this branch, I was transferred immediately to the Orbost (far-eastern Victoria) branch to replace the teller on leave. The journey on my 100cc steed took many hours, not assisted whenever I struck a headwind. I arrived to be met by the curious stares of the locals; clearly someone new was in town. As arranged by the bank, I was put up in the town's hostel and presented myself for work the following morning, where I seemed to be viewed by customers as something of a curiosity. During my three-week stay, the town was one day surrounded and cut off by bushfires, followed a day or two later by floods that also cut off the town, as the single bridge into and out of the town was submerged.

Although I made some friends at Orbost, I wasn't unhappy to be moving on. Future stints included working in the rural towns of Terang, Lancefield, and Bannockburn, where I felt I had stepped back many decades, as the bank's telephone, attached to a wall, required hand cranking to reach the operator.

Glenferrie Road and Firearms

Finally, I received a transfer to take up a more stable position as the number-one teller at the large Glenferrie Road branch in inner-eastern Melbourne. There, my responsibilities included arriving for work well before business hours to open the large walk-in bank vault, fitted with dual highly sensitive combination wheels. Once opened, I removed my pistol and ammunition, in readiness for the business day. I then took out my and the other tellers' cash trays, which required checking against the previous day's close of business balances.

During my three years with the CBA, no written or verbal instructions regarding firearms were ever provided. Only twice was I offered firearm training. Initially, this took place in the weapons range deep in the bank's underground vaults at its Collins Street, Melbourne, head office. There, we fired a clip of six live rounds at circular paper targets. The noise was deafening, not assisted by the lack of ear protection.

The next practice session took place at the Geelong rifle range. Tellers from other banks also attended, all of us under the supervision of a senior police officer. Practice consisted of firing live rounds at a black paper disc, about a metre in diameter, set up on a wooden easel roughly ten metres from the firing position.

The police officer began by demonstrating his prowess with his huge handgun; someone suggested it was a Magnum. We were duly impressed and intimidated at the same time. Following his demonstration, he picked up a pot of glue and patched his bullet holes with small paper discs, expecting each of us to follow his lead, providing we were lucky enough to hit the target.

Soon it was the turn of a non-CBA teller. He abruptly raised his pistol, shut his eyes tight, and emptied his clip in the general direction of the target. He missed it completely but successfully struck the glue pot, sending it flying. The rest of us, the police officer included, scattered in what we hoped was a safe direction. Luckily, only the glue pot was injured.

Armed bank robberies in and around Melbourne during the early 1970s remained relatively common, several occurring not far from the CBA Glenferrie Road branch. In a neighbouring suburb, a teller (not CBA) had been shot when arriving at his branch to open it for the day. This incident put us on edge, and we closely scrutinised any nonregular customers entering our branch.

CBA tellers remained confused regarding any actions expected of us in the event of an armed robbery. The teller-customer interface was open at this time, separated only by a flimsy set of aluminium bars above the wooden teller's station. Automatic, teller-activated security screens were not fitted until decades later. During my time there, our incumbent manager took some leave, to be replaced by a relieving manager. To our surprise, he appeared from his office one day and announced that if we were held up, he would do all the shooting; then without further ado, he returned to his office, shutting his door. Thankfully, we were not robbed during his time with us.

At Glenferrie Road, all four tellers kept our designated pistols loaded, stored on a wooden shelf just below the counter and pointed in the direction of unwitting customers, separated only by a plywood sheet, always with the safety catch on. The branch's pistols were not serviced during my time there, and some of the ammunition had turned green through oxidization; it may well have misfired (or not fired at all) if a shot were required. Fortunately, no robberies occurred during my time at Malvern, although a competitor's branch was held up on a Thursday, which was the regular aged pension and teacher pay day. The perpetrator no doubt hoped to take advantage of this, anticipating getting away with a large haul of cash. He arrived at the branch dressed in drag but was quickly recognised as one of the bank branch's own staff members.

2

Moving On

I knew within a year or two that I was not destined for a long-term banking career, and in 1972, then aged twenty, I left to take on other challenges. I took up a position with a small manufacturing company that produced steel louvres designed to serve as window shades. The company's owner submitted a quotation to install louvres to all seven floors of the north-facing windows of the Royal Women's Hospital, just outside the Melbourne central business district. His bid was successful, and the fitting of the louvres was left to my colleague and I, with a vague promise of a bonus upon completion. Neither of us had any experience or qualifications for this type of work; in effect, we should have at least possessed "scaffolding tickets." Occupational health and safety was not a key consideration for employers at this time.

When we arrived at the site, we found only the scaffolding's steel-pipe framework in place, up to the seventh floor. Moving up from floor to floor required us to climb the pipes and lift long, heavy timber boards up onto each successive level. The narrow boards served as a work platform, but safety harnesses were not provided. Somehow, we managed to complete the work, which became increasingly terrifying as we climbed higher. Not surprisingly, the promised bonus never materialised.

Shortly after completing this job, I was offered a position with an English-based company that manufactured and distributed self-tapping fasteners. I accepted the position and soon discovered that my new manager was sharing a romantic liaison with his secretary. As there were only four full-time staff members, their relationship was difficult to conceal. The manager would sometimes ask me to make excuses regarding his whereabouts should his wife call whilst he was out and about with his secretary.

My tasks included sales, product promotion, and delivery of fasteners requiring zinc or cadmium electroplating. The company seemed to be constantly struggling, and its future seemed uncertain. It was during this time that I applied to Peninsula Ambulance Service (PAS) for the position of ambulance officer (AO). As I discovered soon after, this was fortunate, as the Australian arm of the English company closed down shortly after I left.

As a young adult, I had taken an interest in understanding the geopolitics that led to the Vietnam conflict, aware too that I was eligible for conscription into the Australian Army, which usually meant serving in Vietnam. Fighting in Vietnam continued into 1970, resulting in the unrelenting suffering of the Vietnamese people and those of neighbouring countries. I had read and been disturbed by English author Bertrand Russell's book on the subject, in which he exposed the real motivations behind the conflict. I became involved with the Vietnam Moratorium Campaign protest movement in Melbourne, part of a worldwide effort aimed at pressuring those in power to end the conflict and withdraw all fighting forces. The protest movement culminated in the 1970 Melbourne Moratorium, when 75,000 people marched peacefully down Bourke Street. I have no doubt that this event, along with similar protests around the globe, contributed to the end of hostilities.

Later, I joined Amnesty International and wrote many letters to foreign leaders (usually dictators), urging the release of persecuted prisoners, often facing imminent execution. Perhaps these efforts and my Vietnam Moratorium campaign activities reflected an inherent altruistic leaning.

I do know that I felt a strong desire to help people. Perhaps a career in the ambulance service might fulfil this desire, although I had no concept of what this might entail.

In 1977, being completely ignorant of Victorian ambulance services, I applied initially at the LaTrobe Street headquarters of what was then Ambulance Service Melbourne (ASM). I was interviewed but asked where I lived. When I replied, "Frankston," the response was, "Well, what are you doing here? You should be applying to Peninsula Ambulance Service in Frankston." I had not realised that a separate ambulance service existed in my area; I filled out an application at the Frankston PAS headquarters early in 1977.

PAS was amalgamated with ASM in 1989, becoming Metropolitan Ambulance Service

In May 1977, when I was twenty-five, I was both excited and daunted when PAS accepted my application. I joined a group of ten other recruits. I came late to the group, as I filled a position recently vacated by a PAS ambulance officer who had left to join Victoria Police. I was to be Service Number 107 (numbers being given consecutively to PAS operational staff since its beginnings). Most people do not like to be identified by number, but I soon discovered that two of my new colleagues were particularly proud of their assigned numbers, 83 (ambulance code for a deceased patient) and, of course, 69.

As the initial intake of the ten students AOs in my group had commenced their training with ASM student AOs, and as there was an operational requirement, I was immediately teamed up with an experienced AO who also my designated training officer (TO), and we became an operational crew.

▍ Student Ambulance Officer

The rest of my group had been issued with white overalls to wear whilst training; however, these were not appropriate for operational work. PAS' storeman provided me with what was available as uniform in my size: an unmarked navy blue vinyl jacket and a pair of boots; the remainder of my "uniform" being the clothes I had arrived in for work. This situation continued until I began formal training with other Victorian AO students in August 1977 at the Richmond training rooms. No one at PAS commented on my ad hoc uniform, and so I assumed that I was not the first to begin his ambulance career this way.

My initial informal training was provided by my TO, Warren Green, and conducted either during actual cases or in the downtime in between. Warren debriefed each case with me and familiarised me with all standard ambulance equipment carried on the truck, a two-bed Ambulance General Purpose (AGP). Despite my lack of knowledge and experience, we were despatched on a turn basis with other crews, regardless of case type. I tried to absorb all the new learning that came my way but remained highly anxious, hoping that I was meeting Warren's expectations.

An aerial view of PAS Frankston headquarters, circa 1982, looking east. Just visible at the bottom, right of centre, can be seen the flagpole and the PAS flag, raised each morning by one of the nightshift AOs. I took this photograph from the Angel of Mercy helicopter whilst returning to its base at Tyabb Airfield.

3

Student Ambulance Officer

I soon found that, unlike my previous occupations, no two ambulance shifts were alike, each case presenting new experiences and learnings. Exposure to and interactions with patients, their families, hospitals, and clinics provided an extended informal education, which expanded my knowledge of the wider patient health care chain. It was also plainly evident that my past work experiences in no way prepared me for operational ambulance work, which was clearly a very different and unique profession.

I found Warren to be a compassionate, noncomplaining individual who must have despaired on many occasions being crewed with such a green recruit, being also aware that he was largely responsible for my safety and wellbeing. The very first case we were despatched on was the transfer of a vehicle crash patient from Geelong Hospital to Frankston Hospital, nearer to the patient's residence. This was an unusual case, as I realised when the operations manager emerged from his office as we departed PAS headquarters and called out, "You know, you don't get these sort of jobs every day."

As I had not yet undergone any form of formal emergency driver training, Warren drove all emergency cases requiring the use of lights (beacons) and sirens, known as Signal 8s. Warren was an exceptionally safe and skilful driver with whom I was never alarmed—only by the actions of other road users. My role as the crew "jockey" was to watch his blind side whenever we entered intersections on Signal 8 cases, especially when the traffic lights were red. If I deemed it safe for him to proceed, I was required to call out, "Clear," or "Roger."

Warren introduced me to the absolute PAS patient care rule: We were required to lift each and every patient, regardless of their mobility or medical condition. Even when we deemed it safe, we were not permitted to allow a patient to take a few steps towards our stretcher, which we always positioned as close to the patient as possible. Each patient was lifted employing the "fore and aft" method, requiring one of us to reach behind the patient and lock both hands over the patient's wrists while the other AO lifted the patient's legs with one arm, the other under the patient's lower back. A patient's weight or dimensions didn't factor, as the lifting rule was sacrosanct. Whilst it was praiseworthy that PAS management put the patient's welfare first, it is highly likely that adhering to this rule contributed to future chronic back and knee injuries, which most of us acquired over the years.

Peninsula Ambulance Service provided prehospital care to the citizens of and visitors to the entire Mornington Peninsula, extending to include suburbs as far north as Mordialloc, east to beyond Pakenham, and southeast to as far as Foster. Melbourne, Victoria's state capital, is at the top centre of the map.

The following excerpt is from the *Welcome to Peninsula Ambulance Service* booklet, provided to all new operational recruits. It definitively defines PAS' operational boundaries. ASM and PAS did not encroach into each other's operational zones, sometimes to the detriment of patients requiring ambulance care who happened to live or needed assistance close to the borders. A rare exception occurred in 1986, when PAS was asked to despatch crews to support ASM when the Victoria Police headquarters were bombed in Russell Street, Melbourne. I was part of a crew despatched to this incident from Frankston, on a Signal 8.

> **Peninsula Ambulance Service Boundary**
>
> Modialloc bridge up Boundary Road to Clayton Road, North in Clayton Road to North Road, East in North Road Continuing over Princes Highway into Wellington Road, East along Wellington Road to Narre Warren East, then in a straight line to Gembrook, from Gembrook follow a straight line to Tynong North across to Heath Hill and then South West through the Junction of the Bass and South Gippsland Highway to the coast of Westernport Bay.

Get the What?

One of my first Signal 8 response cases involved a man, perhaps sixty years of age, who had fallen from a ladder whilst tree pruning. Warren called out for me, "Get the Komesaroff!" At this stage, with my very minimal operational experience, I had no idea what he was asking for. He said, "You know, the thing with the yellow cover!" He was referring to the Komesaroff portable oxygen resuscitator which could provide oxygen therapy, oxygen-driven airway suction, and pain relief. It was stored behind the jockey seat, protected by a bright yellow vinyl cover.

Looking back, I was lucky to be rostered with Warren as my TO, as he was exceedingly patient (despite my myriad questions) and not easily shaken in traumatic situations. I appreciated him all the more when in a relatively few years, I found myself in his situation, training and looking out for my first student AO.

How to Debog an Ambulance

Ambulance work often requires rapid decision making and innovation. Such was the case when Warren and I had just completed a routine transport case to a city hospital and were called via radio to urgently meet the PAS Angel of Mercy helicopter. It was due to land shortly at Fawkner Park, Prahran, opposite the Alfred Hospital. The park was one of the helicopter landing sites PAS routinely used across Melbourne and

Mornington Peninsula. We were close enough to drive our ambulance into the park, but this required us to retrieve the key to release the chain across the park's entrance from the hospital clerk's office.

Having done this and dropped the chain, we drove forward, scanning the landing site ahead for nearby park patrons, who often had dogs. It was quickly evident as we moved onto the grass surface that recent rain had left the ground soft. Suddenly, the rear tyres dug in, leaving us bogged a short distance from the landing site. It was then that we heard the familiar sound of helicopter blades beating the air. Thinking quickly, Warren decided to remove all our clean patient linen and force it under the rear tyres, hopefully giving us some improvised traction. Fortunately this worked, and we shoved the muddy linen into a side locker. Our timing was perfect, as the Angel landed moments later, completely unaware of our recent predicament.

Unexpected Trauma

With only a few weeks of operational experience, Warren and I were returning from a late evening Frankston to Melbourne patient transfer, travelling along St. Kilda Road. The traffic lights turned red as we approached Commercial Road, but on the other side of the intersection, we could see the silhouettes of a group of people gathered on the roadway. The lights turned, and our headlights picked up a shape on the road and a large motorcycle laying nearby on its side. We realised quickly that the shape was a person lying motionless on the road. Strangely, the bystanders were watching from a distance, away from the person.

We got out and approached, finding a young woman lying on her back, unconscious. Her abdomen had been completely torn open with her bowels exposed, presumably caused as she was struck by the motorcycle's handle. There was no time to adjust ourselves to the sight of her gross injuries, and we acted quickly; fortunately, we were only two hundred metres from the Alfred Hospital.

All AGPs of the time carried what were known as mines dressings, comprising a cotton pad attached to a long bandage. These came in various sizes and were a throwback to World War I military shell dressings. The pad of the largest mines dressing carried was about thirty centimetres square, usually large enough to accommodate most large, open wounds. We applied two or three of these, which quickly disappeared into her open abdomen. Fortunately, there was little active bleeding from the wound, which we covered with clean towels, lifted her onto our stretcher, and transported her the short distance to hospital. As I recall, the patient did not survive.

As my experiences grew, I found that bystanders, either appalled at what they were witnessing or unaware of what to do, would usually stand back some distance from critically ill patients. Whenever we approached a scene where bystanders were reacting in this way, it invariably indicated serious injury or death.

Usually, when despatched on Signal 8 cases, we were provided with brief details of the case type, such as MCA (motor car accident) or SOB (short of breath). En route to a case, there was usually some time to mentally prepare ourselves and consider treatment options relevant to the case given. In the case described above, known as a field-created event, this did not occur, and we had to adjust our thoughts and actions immediately to the meet the patient's needs.

Witness to Trauma

Much of our shift times were spent travelling to and from cases, hospitals, clinics, and patient residences. It was inevitable then that occasionally we would come upon incidents such as described above. Such was the case during a day shift when we were sent from Frankston headquarters to provide cover in the Dandenong area, as all local crews were busy. We were approaching the Dandenong central business district, not under Signal 8 conditions, and stopped at a red light. I was driving and happened to glance into the rear vision mirror, noticing a vehicle approaching rapidly with clearly insufficient time to stop before reaching the lights. Luckily, there was a free lane beside us, and the vehicle sped through, continuing up to the next intersection, where again the lights were red. The vehicle's brake lights did not come on, and it ploughed at speed into the rear of another vehicle waiting at the lights.

We sat in stunned silence for a moment and then switched on our beacons and accelerated up to the scene. We undertook a quick assessment of the single occupant of the vehicle that had been speeding, finding an elderly female, unconscious. The vehicle struck in the rear held two occupants, a mother and her teenage daughter, who was trapped in what remained of the vehicle's rear. We provided a situation report (sitrep) via radio to our PAS controllers and requested attendance of the MICA crew, who fortunately were also in the Dandenong area.

We split up, my colleague attending to the mother and daughter. The elderly patient had not sustained any obvious traumatic injuries; however, she was in cardiorespiratory arrest (i.e., without a heartbeat and not breathing). I undid her seat belt, slid her onto the roadway, and began cardiopulmonary resuscitation (CPR), the hard road surface providing the firm base necessary to provide effective chest compressions. The MICA crew soon arrived and attempted a resuscitation, which ultimately was unsuccessful. It appeared that the patient had probably suffered a cerebrovascular accident (CVA), more commonly referred to as stroke, leaving her unable to lift her foot from the accelerator or apply the vehicle's brakes. The driver of the other vehicle was unhurt, but her daughter had suffered significant lower back injuries.

4

Who Were We?

All AOs in PAS, ASM, and across Victoria in the 1970s were male. PAS AOs came from many backgrounds. Some had been tradesmen, several were ex-Navy (who invariably made up the tidiest stretchers), and a few were deep sea divers; others came to the ambulance service following varied employment and life experiences. Outside of the operational spheres of ASM and PAS, the remainder of Victoria was served by sixteen independent, regional ambulance services, each with its own superintendent, overseen by the state health department.

At PAS, perhaps 10 percent of AOs had begun their careers as ambulance cadets, starting at what would now be considered the startlingly young age of sixteen or seventeen. In 1977, the age range of PAS AOs was roughly between seventeen and fifty, with a consequent variation in maturity levels; all, however, were committed to providing optimum patient care.

Nicknames at PAS were rife, the origins of some no one seemed to recall, even the recipients. Examples included "Dingbat," "Gumboots," "Piles," "Fingerbone," "Blackjack," "Bucky Beaver," "Spider," "Mongrel," and my favourite, "Did I" (so called for his habit of frequently forgetting things, e.g., "Did I leave my jumper in the mess room?"). Whilst some nicknames reflected personalities, others were concocted from family names; mine was variously "Shazzam," "Viking," or "Erik the Red" (in deference to my Danish heritage on my mother's side). I didn't object to my nicknames, as for me, it indicated a level of acceptance by my colleagues.

We also gave nicknames to some of our unwitting medical colleagues, including doctors, nurses, and surgeons. Some were very imaginative, even evocative; for example, we called a well-known gastro intestinal surgeon "Elbows," as he was often known to be elbows deep in a patient's abdominal cavity during surgery. Perhaps taking a lazier approach to giving nicknames, we called one of the Frankston Hospital orderlies "Igor," as his responsibilities extended to mortuary duties.

A few of our regular patients also received our attention, including an elderly male who was transported at least weekly to a city clinic; no matter how well he got to know each of us, he always reminded us to take along his "two bags and two sticks"—and thus he was known.

A handful of PAS' more senior AOs had reputations as heavy drinkers and in all probability could be classified as alcoholics. Occasionally, one would arrive for his shift reeking strongly of alcohol, the smell of which he was usually unaware. Of course, they were a potential danger to us, patients, and other road users. We, however, looked upon them as colleagues, and whilst it was embarrassing, we would always take them aside and suggest that they return home (sometimes via taxi). We would then advise the shift senior station officer (SSO) that our colleague had arrived for work unwell and could not begin his shift. In my experience, alcohol-affected AOs approached in this way always followed our advice. Whether or not the SSO suspected anything mattered little to us; we only sought to protect our colleagues.

The various personalities and character traits of PAS AOs made for a colourful working environment. One of our colleagues, for example, had a reputation as somewhat of a hypochondriac. He carried an extensive array of prescription and over-the-counter medication in his vinyl AO carry bag. This habit benefitted his colleagues, as he always had a remedy at hand for whatever ailment we might have been suffering.

Between cases, during our downtime, we tended to congregate in the Frankston headquarters mess room, where we talked shop, played cards, or watched TV. Many AOs were chain smokers, including a few pipe smokers. Smoking in the mess room was a long-established and accepted practice; the smoke, though, was at times so thick that it hung cloud-like at eye level. No one had heard of passive smoking at the time; besides which, the regular smokers would not be denied their habit.

Jargon

As student AOs, we quickly absorbed and repeated the jargon peculiar to ambulance and, more generally, hospital environments. For example, our radio controllers despatched us to motor vehicle accidents, referring to them only as MCAs. Between us, however (but never used over the radio), we referred to them as "prangs"—perhaps deriving from the vernacular used by World War II Royal Air Force pilots when referring to aircraft crashes. Falls in the elderly often resulted in fractures of the femur, close to the hip, described medically as a fractured neck of femur, or more commonly, just "NOF." Patients complaining of indefinite abdominal symptoms we referred to as "MGAs," short for Mediterranean Guts Ache (political correctness was a concept far in the future). We referred to inebriated patients who had suffered a fall resulting in injury as "PFO" (pissed and fell over).

Culture and Attitudes

Every workplace, seemingly regardless of type, develops a culture peculiar to it, influenced perhaps by the nature of the work and workers' ages, gender, characters, location, and other factors. In the case of PAS, various subcultures existed, peculiar to the branch location and the personalities of those permanently rostered there. AOs usually rostered at the Frankston headquarters, for example, were often critical of the skills and clinical decisions made by experienced station officers at peripheral branches. We tended to believe that they possessed a "load and go" mentality, favouring rapid transport over patient treatment. With hindsight, this view was usually unfair, as these colleagues frequently responded alone, often on an exhausting on-call basis. Peripheral branch SOs usually operated in isolation, unless they called for crew backup. In circumstances where backup crews were unavailable, or the time delay in waiting for backup might be detrimental to their patient, they sometimes loaded the patient and drove directly to hospital. If lucky, they might second a police officer or firefighter to drive the ambulance, leaving them free to attend to the patient. In the end, in most cases, our remote criticism was unjustified and was tantamount to a type of indirect bullying. No doubt, on occasion, some of our comments reached our peripheral colleagues, probably resulting in unwarranted and unnecessary psychological harm. Most of us were guilty of this behaviour at one time or another, something I certainly learned to regret.

In the prevailing culture amongst AOs at the Frankston headquarters, discussions of attendance at traumatic cases was limited to the circumstances of what had happened; no one disclosed how events made them feel. This was largely because crews returning from such cases came back into the all-male environment of the mess room, where usually a number of other crews were waiting to be despatched. To discuss feelings in this context was considered to be unacceptable and a sign of weakness. A crew returning from a serious vehicle crash might simply be asked "What did you get?", to which the response may have been, "One Charlie and an 83" (one critically injured patient and one deceased). Little further information was given or sought, and there the discussion would end.

Opportunities for the service and AOs to learn from cases involving multiple patients were limited or lost altogether. At such cases, things could and did go wrong, particularly regarding communication, both verbal and via radio. Formal debriefs, including all staff involved in the case, aimed at understanding what went wrong and potentially leading to improvements, were not conducted, hence mistakes were repeated. Understandably, the costs associated with bringing crews together following such cases to conduct formal debriefs would be significant; however, it would have been worthwhile.

Ambulance Drivers

Many of our older patients from this period referred to us as "ambulance drivers," no doubt based on their understanding or actual experiences with military ambulances during both world wars. The term rankled with us, as we considered ourselves to be professional ambulance officers, capable of and responsible for doing far more for our patients than providing just transport. We dealt with this perceived slight on our profession with self-deprecating humour by referring to each other as "driver." In a similar self-deprecating but far more disturbing manner, non-MICA AOs referred to themselves as "road scum," reflecting a cynical view that they regarded themselves as sitting far below MICA officers on the clinical scale.

Whenever student AOs worked alongside our MICA colleagues, we were often left in awe of their skills, capabilities, and knowledge, frequently resulting in dramatic improvements in a patient's condition. It was always a revelation to us when MICA opened their drug box or airway bag, displaying items beyond our comprehension. We always thought twice before requesting MICA assistance in the field, as we hated to hear their refrain: "Well, what did you call us for?" In my later MICA days, I recalled this and never repeated this demeaning phrase to my non-MICA colleagues.

Some AOs were of the view that MICA officers saw themselves as elite, demonstrated by what they viewed as arrogant behaviour. On the whole, this was not my experience, although one or two MICA officers were aloof and remote. I felt that this was more a reflection of their personalities. I found most MICA officers forthcoming and encouraging when approached with questions. I remembered this when I became MICA qualified in 1984 and strived to make AOs feel included in the patient treatment decision-making process, including whether or not to continue resuscitation efforts.

As junior AOs, we were keen to attend emergency cases, where our new skills and knowledge could be put to the test. A degree of envy sometimes crept in if another crew was despatched to a potentially challenging case, and sometimes there were complaints if a crew believed our controllers had assigned a crew to such a case out of turn.

To be fair, the PAS controllers had a difficult job, managing their resources without the aid of current-day technology, such as GPS location. Instead, they relied on crew availability at branches, geographically closest to a case location. Where crews were not at branch, controllers called crews via radio, anticipating, based on their last or current case, that they may be nearest to a given case location. As the sole PAS MICA resource, the MICA crew were often required concurrently at more than one case. If MICA was at a hospital, in the process of providing patient handover, it was common for a PAS controller to contact them via the direct line to the Casualty Department (later to become the Accident and Emergency Department) and urge the crew to "clear" as soon as possible to respond to another time-critical case. I felt this pressure many times during my early days on the PAS MICA unit. It was not unusual to be providing hospital staff with a complicated patient handover only to be pressured to clear to respond to another potential MICA case.

A photo illustrating the cramped confines of the original PAS control room, from where all PAS operational resources were managed around the clock. The controllers were also responsible for receiving 000 emergency calls. Alf Greaves is on the phone, and the late Peter Ballard is in the foreground.

Other Characters

The PAS headquarters complex at Frankston consisted of a large garage/workshop, car wash bay, storeroom, control room, mess room/kitchen, locker room, training room, and administrative staff offices. Some of the non-AO staff were interesting characters, including our cleaner. He was extremely gullible, a trait we took advantage of for our own amusement. One day, he appeared from his toilet cleaning duties, clutching a clear plastic bag, containing what appeared to be plant material. He had found it taped inside one of the toilet bowls; very excited by his find, he ran into our kitchen, calling out, "Marijooaana!" We looked closely at the contents, which very clearly were nothing more than pine-tree needles. He'd been had again. We had no prior knowledge of the prank but knew immediately who was behind it.

The cleaner routinely reported to a particular senior station officer; he approached him one day, requesting to take a day off on the following Friday. The SSO replied, "Sorry, I can't do that, as it will give you a long weekend, but you can take the Monday off." The cleaner was wise enough not to quibble and enjoyed his long weekend off.

Our chief mechanic was a middle-aged man with a perpetually cranky disposition. He was nicknamed "Punchy," and it was alleged that he would throw spanners at AOs who had damaged one of his mechanical charges. For a long period and much to our disgust, he had the habit of coming into our kitchen and taking our daily newspaper (paid for by the AO social club) to read in the toilet. We all complained about his unhygienic habit, but he remained unmoved. Finally, someone struck on a means of fighting back by putting the double front page of the current newspaper edition around the main contents of a much earlier edition. This had the desired effect, as after a few minutes, we could hear him swearing from the toilets. Eventually, he gave up, defeated.

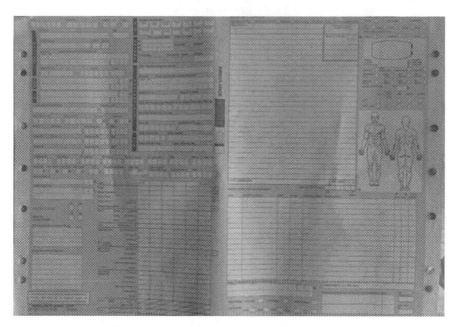

The original A3 sized paper-based Patient Care Record, carbonised in triplicate, since replaced with an electronic tablet.

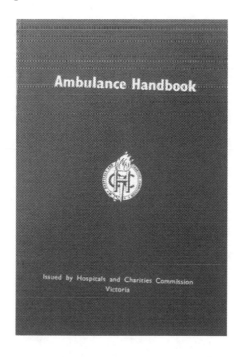

Erik Schanssema

The handbook pictured above was provided to all Victorian AOs by the Hospitals and Charities Commission (now the Victorian Department of Human Services) as a general ready reference and as a supplement to internal ambulance training. The pages from the handbook show the following:

- the fault finding chart in the event of the ambulance engine failing to start
- information regarding assessments of specific patient injuries

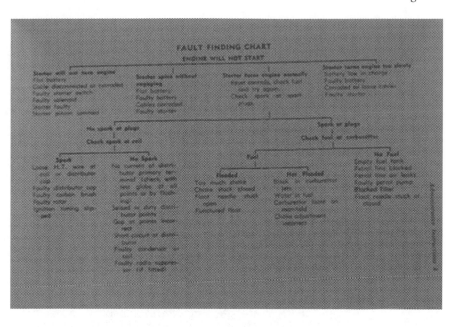

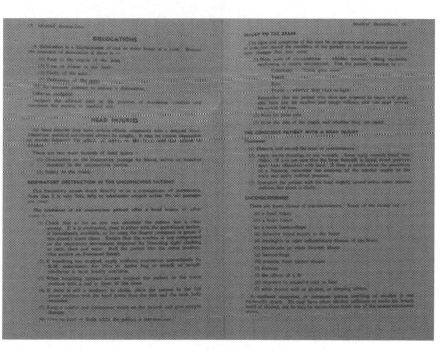

5

Equipment

Ambulance General Purpose (AGP)

In the late 1970s and 1980s, PAS emergency ambulances were based on the Ford F100 light commercial truck, fitted with a fibreglass shell which comprised the patient treatment area and the transport module. These were fitted with double rear doors and later with a single lift-up door, much favoured by crews, as it offered some protection from the elements when loading or unloading patients. Each vehicle carried a main stretcher (colloquially referred to as the bed), fitted with folding legs. The early model of this stretcher suffered from occasional, unexpected, sudden failure of the leg-locking mechanism. Many AOs sustained injuries when stretcher collapse occurred with a patient on board, as the instinctive reaction is to clutch at the stretcher handles, in the hope of preventing patient injury.

A second bed consisted of a heavy, legless steel frame fitted with a thick vinyl mattress and small solid wheels. This stretcher, with a patient loaded, had to be lifted from ground level, often requiring four pairs of hands. Two further patient-carrying devices were fitted above the main beds. These were also weighty, constructed of fibreglass, with a concave base, and could be lowered for use midway, suspended by metal hooks from the ambulance ceiling. Generally, these were only employed to carry deceased patients from multiple-fatality incidents back to hospital mortuaries. The concavity served as a resevoir for blood and body fluid.

Unless an AO was vertically challenged, as a few were, it was impossible to stand upright in the rear of the AGPs of the time. Treating a patient whilst mobile was both difficult and potentially dangerous. The AO driving would try to alert his colleague in the rear prior to making sudden manoeuvres, although urgent braking would not allow warning time, resulting in the AO being thrown to the floor, occasionally ending up between the front seats.

In an effort to reduce transport times to hospital, invasive techniques such as insertion of intravenous needles were often carried out whilst mobile. Intubation was usually done prior to transport; however, if required en route to hospital, and due to the risk of misplacement, insertion of endotracheal tubes (ETT), protecting a patient's airway, required stopping the ambulance to safely carry out the procedure.

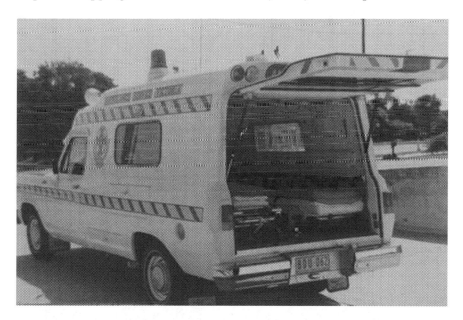

A PAS Ambulance General Purpose, fitted with the preferred single lift-up door. The height of the door when open presented a challenge for shorter AOs, who sometimes had to perform a running jump to reach the handle to pull it down. Inside on the left-hand side is the main stretcher fitted with folding undercarriage. On the right is the spare stretcher.

Cleaning

Until the 1990s, much of the portable equipment and patient treatment devices were nondisposable, requiring manual cleaning between uses. This included the twin, black corrugated rubber oxygen hoses fitted to the Komesaroff oxygen resuscitator, most commonly used during resuscitation attempts, attached to the patient's ETT. The hoses were part of a closed system and were cleaned by soaking in disinfectant, followed by a water rinse. This task was usually done in the hospital Casualty Department's wet area; when complete, we took the hoses out to the ambulance parking bay, where we could often be seen spinning them about, in an effort to air-dry them. Where the hoses had been used at patient residences, we would discreetly use the patient's bathroom to clean up both our gear and ourselves, no doubt resulting in variable infection control levels.

Infection Control

Spot cleaning of blood and body fluid was usually accomplished using Hexol, a pink disinfectant carried by all ambulances of the time, and followed up with a towel. Larger blood and body fluid spills often resulted in the contamination of equipment, stretchers, and ambulance interiors. Cleanup was carried out using whatever hospital disinfectant we could acquire from casualty departments. Major blood and body fluid spills, sometimes mixed with brake fluid, oils, battery acids, or whatever else we may have trodden in, required mopping the vehicle interior with a borrowed hospital bucket and mop. We filled the bucket with hot water and added a good dose of our favoured hospital disinfectant, or whatever happened to be available. During the earlier years, there were no documented ambulance infection control guidelines; nevertheless, we did what we could to keep our vehicles and equipment as clean as possible. As blood and body fluid can seep into unseen areas (e.g., under stretcher rails), occasionally vehicles had to be partially dismantled and professionally cleaned by a contractor.

Finally, at PAS at least, we were required to sweep and mop out the front and rear of our ambulances at the beginning and end of each shift.

Cleaning Can Be Fun

Disposable gloves were not introduced as mandatory wear for AOs attending patients until the early 1980s, when the global fear of HIV/ AIDS increased (refer photo of John Wheeler and me treating an injured motorcyclist sans gloves). Prior to this time, a relatively few of us would liberate handfuls of disposable gloves from hospital casualty departments. For in-field hand cleaning, we used Hexol solution, and if our hands and arms were contaminated with blood and body fluid, we would liberally pour the solution over them, although frequent use sometimes resulted in unwanted skin conditions. Hexol was generally available in casualty departments, including at Frankston Hospital. It was here that a PAS crew, made up of two AOs with reputations for always behaving as gentlemen, were washing up after moving their patient from their stretcher to the hospital bed. As usual, they used the Hexol bottle placed inside a wire cradle and attached to a wall above a casualty department sink; however, the bottle became dislodged and dropped to the floor, spilling its contents. One of the crew innocently asked a nurse, "Is your Hexol slippery?", concerned that others might slip in the spill while they looked for a means to clean it up.

She looked aghast, apparently believing that what she heard was "Is your sex hole slippery?" The misunderstanding was quickly cleared up, and the crew's unblemished reputations were restored, but when they returned to the Frankston mess room and related their embarassment, we collapsed in tears, and the story became legendary.

An example of the PAS checklist forms from the late 1970s listing some of the standard equipment carried on AGPs.

Oxygen and Pain Relief

Oxygen was, of course, fundamental in treating patients suffering from a range of respiratory and other medical conditions. The gas was stored throughout our AGPs in various sized steel cylinders and could be delivered via facemask or twin-prong nasal cannulas. 100 percent oxygen was required at times and could be delivered by the portable Komesaroff oxygen resuscitator via a black inflatable rubber mask connected to twin black rubber hoses. This was a heavy item, essentially an anaesthetic machine based on those found in operating theatres and designed by an anaesthetist of the same name. Built on a stainless steel base to which we attached a C-size oxygen cylinder, we usually just referred to it as the Kommy. It was also designed to allow for oxygen-powered airway suction and as an alternative method of providing pain relief through vapourising the drug Methoxyflurane (generically known as Penthrane). A cannister filled with soda lime crystals was fitted to one end, which absorbed a patient's expired carbon dioxide. The crystals required regular repalcement following use, usually in a cardiorespiratory arrest situation, or when the crystal's colour changed.

Fractures

Fractured femurs (thigh bone) were relatively common in road crashes of the time, particularly front-end collisions and unlucky motorcyclists. Unless the fracture was open, splinting at the crash scene was desired. This was achieved using another heavy steel- based item called the modified Thomas splint. It was a length-adjustable traction device which when properly applied allowed a degree of temporary reduction of the fracture, remaining in place until the patient reached the operating theatre. Its proper use also provided a level of pain relief, as the large thigh muscles returned to their precontracted state.

Suspected limb fractures were surrounded by a plastic sleeve, known as an airsplint, inflatable by mouth (at the time). These served to stabilise the fracture and further protect the injured limb. Patients with suspected cervical fractures were fitted with a hard, partially adjustable vinyl collar. Looking back, these devices probably provided little cervical support and were likely largely ineffective. In cases of suspected spinal fracture, we also secured the patient to our stretcher by improvising with triangular bandages and placing rolled towels on either side of the patient's head/neck, acting as rudimentary restraints.

Patient Extrication

For lifting from floor or roadways with minimal patient movement, we carried a scissors-like contraption that fitted around the patient and closed and locked at the foot end. Alternatively, we employed the Jordan lifting frame, fitted with multiple steel upright pins. Fitted over the patient, flexible vinyl slats could then be slid underneath and attached to the pins, the patient's weight keeping them in place. Both devices were effective but strained our legs and backs, as they were usually lifted from ground level.

A fibreglass spineboard became available in later years, providing another means of lifting, moving, and carrying patients. Depending on a patient's injuries, position, and location within a wrecked vehicle, the spineboard was sometimes an effective tool for patient extrication. Patients in a sitting position with suspected cervical or spinal injury could be secured in situ to the Kendrick Extrication Device (KED) via a long plastic splint, curved for support at neck level. This was secured to the patient with multiple straps. Handles at each side assisted in the patient's final extrication.

A PAS clinical rule required us to record patient observations every fifteen minutes during transport, regardless of the patient's condition, including conscious state, heart and respiratory rates, and blood pressure (BP). Obtaining an accurate BP in a moving vehicle by listening through a stethoscope in a moving, noisy ambulance was difficult. In the case of a patient being hypotensive (low BP), the only way to ensure an accurate assessment was to stop the vehicle. A large dialled sphygmomanometer was fitted in the AGP rear, whilst a handheld portable sphygmo was carried into most case locations. This unit included a standard cuff, suitable for most adult arm circumferences. For those with more substantial arm circumferences, a much longer cuff, irreverently called a "slug" cuff, was available.

The standard stethoscope carried in PAS AGPs was inexpensive and of poor quality. As we became more experienced and increasingly frustrated with this cheap model, most of us privately purchased the far superior Littman stethoscope, although woe betide any AO seen at hospital wearing any type of stethoscope draped over his neck or using it for any other purpose than recording BPs. To do so was seen as an encroachment into the domain of doctors and therefore forbidden. Only MICA officers with their enhanced training and clinical knowledge were permitted broader stethoscope use, such as respiratory assessment.

A rudimentary midwifery kit was carried on all AGPs, containing umbilical clamps, scissors and various dressings, and an APGAR score calculation card, from which we determined the total score reflecting a newborn's health status, based on appearance, pulse, grimace, activity, and respiration. A less-than-optimum score indicated the newborn being in acute distress (if this was not already evident to us).

This photo illustrates the difficult and dangerous environments paramedics sometimes encounter. I am under the train, treating a critically injured patient, struck by the train. In events such as this, we would not hesitate to crawl under a train to reach a patient. Nevertheless, it was always an unnerving experience, as we were not always certain that the train would not move off.

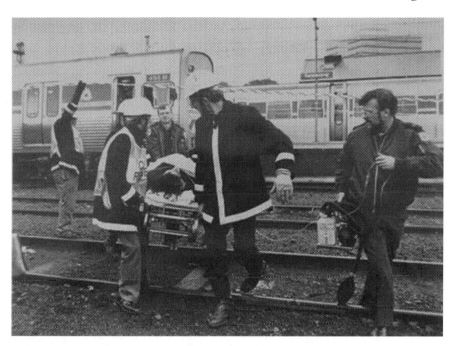

This photo from the same incident shows the Komesaroff oxygen resuscitator being carried and providing oxygen to a critically injured patient who had been struck by a train. Although not required at this stage of the patient's rescue, the inflatable black oxygen bag used to provide ventilatory support is visible in the lower right corner. The soda lime canister used to absorb a patient's expired carbon dioxide (CO_2) is seen just above the oxygen bag. I am at the foot end of the stretcher, having just treated and recovered the patient from under the train. Sadly, this patient, suffering multiple limb amputations, did not survive the short trip to hospital.

We worked by the "transport is treatment" mantra, constantly reinforced by PAS management, reminding us not to "stay and play," rather to move time-critical patients to hospital as soon as safely possible. This did not (and still does not) mean that time-critical patients are "rushed" to hospital, as is so frequently described by the media. Depending on the patient's condition, primary emergency treatment such as airway management, pain relief, arresting haemorrhage, and fracture splinting are best done as part of primary patient care, before transport.

Untreated severe pain may cause unwanted physiological repercussions, such as increased anxiety, heart rate, and blood pressure. Providing early, adequate pain relief is fundamental in providing good patient care.

Non-MICA ambulances of the time carried the potent pain relief drug Methoxyflurane, which was usually self-administered by the patient by inhaling the drug through a plastic tube, into which we had poured the appropriate dose. Pain relief was usually achieved within a few minutes; however, the drug was potent enough to render the patient unconscious for short periods. It also sometimes had the effect of causing a state of euphoria, and patients so affected required a good deal of persuasion to hand back the inhaler. Penthrane (its generic name) has a distinctive odour, similar to Juicy Fruit gum, which was how we introduced it to patients.

To induce vomiting in patients who had overdosed on prescription medication, and only if their conscious state allowed, we encouraged the patient to drink a small cupful of syrup of Ipecac, a viscous liquid. Its effect was rapid, requiring us to be prepared to collect the resultant vomitus in a plastic ice cream container for later examination by medical staff. The concept of this action was to allow doctors to examine the contents to assist in determining the types and quantity of medication consumed. The challenge for us, though, was to arrive at the hospital without any spillage—a much desired outcome. A handful of our colleagues suffered from car sickness, particularly when in the rear of the ambulance and facing to the rear. Holding the ice cream container in a moving, poorly ventilated ambulance, whilst gagging from the smell of the contents and from the effects of car sickness, was quite testing for these individuals.

AGPs also carried so-called "wrecking gear," made up of a small crowbar, a hacksaw, and a type of short-handled axe. These items were for use in accessing and extricating patients trapped in vehicle wreckage. They were ineffective if a patient was thoroughly trapped, for example, legs pinned under a dashboard. In such cases, in the PAS area of operations, we relied on the assistance of the Langwarrin Country Fire Authority (CFA) rescue vehicle, which carried the powerful pneumatic scissors-like device, the "Jaws of Life." At times, we climbed inside a wrecked vehicle, protecting the patient's face with a blanket whilst the Jaws removed the vehicle roof or doors. Any paramedic who has been in this situation will forever remember the sound of the Jaws as it tore and cut through crushed metal, within centimetres of where we were positioned.

Just Like Falling off a Cliff

Viewed from above, Mornington Peninsula appears somewhat like a left-facing boot, jutting into Port Phillip Bay to the west and Westernport Bay to the east . At various points along its length, cliffs rise above many of its beautiful beaches. There are many walking paths above the cliffs, but visitors sometimes stray too close to edges, resulting in falls. For such eventualities, PAS AGPs carried two forty-foot ropes, abseiling carabineers, and hard hats.

To prepare student AOs for such cases, we received training in fundamental abseiling techniques, carried out initially at the Mornington beach cliffs. Fitness varied considerably in my student group. Each of us was required to asbeil down the roughly fifteen-metre drop, alongside PAS Training Officer Gerry Thomas, who would instruct and encourage us as we made our descent. Once safely on the beach, we were required to pull ourselves back to the cliff top via our ropes. The first of our colleagues chosen announced that he had some previous abseiling experience, and before Gerry could stop him, he promptly disappeared over the edge and, with a few bounds, landed safely on the sand. Having witnessed this impressive display, the next candidate positioned himself with his back facing the sea, and perhaps overly encouraged by this demonstration, followed his example, but miscalculated, ending up inverted halfway down the cliff, with one foot caught in a crevasse. Several of us hauled him back to the top, where he sat on the ground, resting his rapidly swelling ankle on a first aid box.

Another of our colleagues was a good deal overweight; he carried the nickname Slim. His weight no doubt assisted his descent, but puffing and panting, he was unable to pull himself back to the top without our assistance.

When my turn arrived, I stood with my back to the beach, Gerry reminding me not to look down and to keep my legs straight. I leant back and walked partway down, then made a couple of jumps before coming to the bottom. I pulled myself back up and, I think, repeated the process.

Making my first unsteady descent down the Mornington beach cliffs.

On a training day, some years later, we had the opportunity to reinforce our abseiling skills, this time from a twenty-metre-high bridge, with nowhere to place our feet. Note the modern nylon ropes compared to the original hemp ropes used during our initial PAS training.

Along with abseiling practice, we were also trained in enclosed environment rescues, including along underground concrete culverts. Partially obscured PAS AO Dick Seaton's (seated) knee is the rope which we used as a guide to descend into the very narrow opening, a most uncomfortable experience for those of us who suffered from claustrophobia.

6

Driving

The Ford F100, adapted for ambulance use, was fundamentally a light commercial truck, not designed for high-speed driving and manoeuvring. Nevertheless, over time and in all weathers, we became acquainted with each of PAS' AGPs, each with its own quirks. Being young men, we favoured the fastest AGPs, which we pushed to their (and our) limits.

One of our colleagues was not satisifed with the speeds we could achieve in our standard AGPs and struck on the idea of inverting the air filter cover, resulting in a significant power boost (however, also dramatically increasing engine noise). Punchy, our humourless chief mechanic, was soon on to us and ensured that the practice was banned.

On open highways, most F100s were capable of speeds over 160 KPH (approximately 100 MPH); ambulance crashes were rare and usually occurred at low speed. We believed that this safety record was due to our familiarity with each AGP, combined with the sheer volume of Signal 8 cases that we drove.

To some degree, we tended to modify our driving behaviour based on the nature of Signal 8 case types; for example, we drove a little bit harder when responding to a time-critical case, such as a cardiac arrest, or to any critical paediatric case. Pushing AGPs to their limits could result in us arriving at a case scene with smoke billowing from red-hot front brakes, sometimes resulting in fire, including in the engine bay.

The distances we travelled on Signal 8 cases across PAS' operational areas varied from a few minutes to up to one hour. The longest cases required great concentration and could leave the driver utterly mentally and physically drained on arrival.

Until the mid-1980s, AGP warning lights and sirens were operated via dashboard toggle switches. The sirens were fitted directly above the driver and jockey, and the repeated "bee-baa" sound would still be ringing in our ears at the end of the shift. Later, a foot switch was fitted to operate the sirens, and there was much excitement as the new Loctronic sirens were progressively fitted to the front of all AGPs. These produced variable tones, identical to Victoria Police and Fire Service emergency vehicles.

The 1976 movie, *Mother, Jugs, and Speed*, a comedy about competing privately run Los Angeles ambulance services, came to Australian television a few years later; given its ambulance theme, it was very popular with us. The movie included a scene where an ambulance crew frightens a group of nuns with their sirens. Gathered in front of the PAS mess room TV, we thought this was hilarious, and a challenge went out to all crews to re-create the scene locally (a difficult challenge, as nuns were a rare sight on the Mornington Peninisula). When not responding to a Signal 8 case, the use of ambulance sirens was forbidden by PAS management. Some weeks later, my colleague and I were driving without a patient on board through the town of Mount Eliza and couldn't believe our luck when ahead of us was a group of nuns about to the cross the street. Unconcerned with PAS management or even divine repercussions, we gave them a short burst of sirens, sending them scurrying, habits flying. How we laughed. On our return to Frankston headquarters, we enjoyed a period of infamy, having completed the challenge. Thankfully, the nuns, by their good graces we assumed, did not make a complaint to PAS.

Public Reaction

Emergency service vehicles using sirens are usually heard before being seen; their directional approach is not always clear to other road users and pedestrians. On the whole, the majority of other road users make every effort to give way to emergency vehicles; however, the reaction and behaviour of some can be dangerous. Some drivers, having seen us suddenly loom up in their rear vision mirror, panic, brake suddenly, and remain in the same traffic lane. Others see an emergency vehicle approaching behind them, and whilst considerate drivers are giving way, they instead seize the opportunity to get that little bit ahead in the traffic by following in our wake. Late one night, we were responding under Signal 8 conditions to yet another suspected heroin overdose. A carload of young fools appeared alongside us and followed us through each red light, finally only thwarted when they spotted a police car waiting for us at the case location.

7

Mortuaries

Frankston and Dandenong and District Hospitals had built-in mortuaries and, by arrangement with PAS, would accept our deceased patients. The arrangement was usually limited to acceptance of deceased patients who had suffered an unexpected death, including those killed through trauma and therefore requiring a coronial investigation to determine cause of death (under the Victorian Coroner's Act).

Regardless of the extent of a deceased patient's injuries, including decapitation, AOs could not legally certify death. Each deceased patient arriving at a hospital mortuary had to be examined by and certified deceased by a casualty department doctor. Junior doctors were often assigned this task, and before examinig the patient, we would try to prepare them for what they were about to see. Deceased patients with massive traumatic injuries usually only received a cursory examination; lifting the sheet covering the patient was often enough.

I recall arriving at Frankston Hospital with a number of "83s," all young people killed in a major MCA. We had not had the time or facilities to clean ourselves up and entered the casualty department heavily blood-stained, to request the mortuary key and a doctor to certify our patients. We returned to our ambulance with a young doctor, who found blood leaking from beneath the side door and spilling onto the parking bay and along the gutter, in full view of the passing public.

On another occasion, we arrived again at Frankston Hospital with a deceased middle-aged male patient, who had been the sole occupant of a vehicle that had struck a tree at high speed. We went through the usual motions of seeking out the mortuary key and asking the sister in charge to find a doctor. The mortuary was unlocked externally, beside the ambulance parking bay. Unlocking the door, we were met by the sight of Igor, the hospital porter, stripping the contents of a patient's bowels, which he had draped over his shoulder, into a stainless steel bucket. I still recall the sight, sickening sound, and the smell. Although postmortem tables were part of the mortuary's facilities, we had never before encountered such a scene, leaving us both feeling disturbed.

8

Angel of Mercy

The Angel of Mercy was a single-engined Bell Jetranger helicopter operated under contract by PAS. It was adapted from its usual four-seat passenger transport configuration to be fitted with an aluminium stretcher along the left side of the aircraft, a patient's feet extending into the cockpit, beside the pilot, positioned on the right. PAS was, at the time, the first ambulance service in the world to operate a helicopter for patient transport, usually non-time-critical patients flying between Mornnigton Peninsula hospitals and major Melbourne hospitals. The Angel carried much of the same equipment as a standard AGP; however, its confined interior allowed for only limited patient access by the AO, seated to the right of the patient and directly behind the pilot. To provide any patient treatment required the AO to turn to his left, remaining restrained by his lap belt, and with only the patient's upper body accessible. Performing single-person CPR in this setting was impossible. The AO and pilot were separated only by a Komesaroff oxygen resuscitator, fitted at the AO's eye level. The advantage of the helicopter's speed was occasionally undermined if a patient's condition rapidly deteriorated during flight, leaving the pilot with the single option of rapidly locating a safe landing site and call for road ambulance backup.

One of our colleagues complained bitterly that he had never been chosen to fly in the Angel; he badgered the PAS controllers, who finally relented. He was thrilled and tasked with accompanying a patient on a routine transport flight. Arriving at Tyabb Airfield, he duly reported to the pilot and strapped himself into position, placed his headset on, and indicated to the pilot that he was ready. Barely above the ground, he rewarded the pilot with an explosive vomit, through the gaps in the Kommy and onto the pilot's back. The flight was aborted and the AO subsequently permanently grounded. Many of the Angel's pilot were ex-military, having flown helicopters during the Vietnam conflict. We were never told how the pilot reacted, but it isn't difficult to surmise.

Tyabb Airshow

I flew on the Angel on many occasions, including most memorably directly over the Melbourne Cricket Ground during a Victorian Football League (VFL, now AFL) Grand Final premiership match. The Angel was stored on a pallet in a hangar at Tyabb Airfield, requiring a small tractor to move it out to its take-off position. When required for a flight, PAS controllers contacted the pilot by phone, who would have the aircraft warmed up and ready to fly, usually within fifteen minutes. This roughly equalled the time required for the nominated AO to drive from PAS Frankston headquarters to the airfield, sometimes under Signal 8 conditions. Having a lifelong passion for aviation, I was very pleased to be assigned to the Angel on the day of the annual Tyabb Airshow. We were to give a flight display, combined with a mock vehicle rescue. A colleague drove me to Tyabb, and we had only just arrived when I was given an actual case, an urgent case. I was advised that a young man had dived off the pier at Queenscliff into shallow water and was found floating, unconscious.

We took off immediately, tracking down the east coast of Port Phillip Bay, then crossing the water at the bay's entrance, known as the Rip for its fast-flowing tidal changes. We landed on the beach, adjacent to the pier. The patient was a seventeen-year-old male who had been taken as gently as possible by swimmers and laid out on the sand. He was now conscious, alert, and complaining of significant neck pain, unable to move or feel his legs. I provided him with pain relief and applied the necessary cervical splinting in preparation for the flight to hospital.

With the patient now "packaged," I happened to glance over at the Angel. The pilot had left the engine running, as was usual practice, but the aircraft's vibrations were causing it to sink into the dry sand, which the tail rotor was now spraying in an arc. I alerted the pilot, who sprinted to the Angel, climbed in, and lifted it off to a nearby location, where the sand was firm. We loaded the patient and flew north, heading directly to the Austin Hospital, renowned for its excellent spinal unit. I was pleased to later receive a commendation for my treatment and management of the patient from the unit's director.

We lifted off from the Austin Hospital's landing site and headed back to Tyabb, where the airshow was still under way. Our position in the flying program had to be adjusted, but as we approached, a cloud base had formed over the area, at about a thousand feet. The pilot suddenly spotted parachutists in our path, popping out from under the cloud base. He veered off, and we returned for our display when all was clear. The pilot performed a high-speed low-level pass along the length of Tyabb's grass airfield, beating it up as I waved to the crowd: a great way to finish what turned out to be a very interesting shift.

The Jesus Bolt

Some of my colleagues had no interest whatsoever in flying in the Angel, the standard joke being that it only took the "Jesus" bolt (the bolt that secured the main rotor shaft to the rotor) to give way, rendering the aircraft uncontrollable, ending in an inevitable crash and consequently a rendezvous with Jesus. With my passion for all things flying, I wasn't concerned and particularly loved the sensation of lifting off and the tight turns the pilot made in preparation for landing, which left us seemingly motionless, looking straight down at the ground.

One day, I was despatched to Tyabb for the air transport of a patient from Frankston Hospital to the Alfred Hospital, just south of Melbourne. As we lifted off from the park directly behind the hospital, I noticed dark clouds coming across Port Phillip Bay to our left. The patient was not time-critical and required only routine monitoring during the flight. The return flight was smooth, although the weather was quickly closing in. The PAS controllers had despatched a crew to retrieve me when we landed back at Frankston Hospital. I spotted them as we approached, waving in what I assumed was a friendly greeting, and I waved back. There was no direct communication between crews and the Angel, nor did the crew have the time to return to their ambulance radio (no portables either, at this time). They had noticed that in the deteriorating weather, the boom of a crane used in the construction of the hospital's new boiler room had broken loose and was swinging about in the wind, close to where the pilot was manoeuvring to land. By this time, we had landed, and the crew explained that they were desperately trying to warn us; they were not being friendly at all.

Erik Schanssema

The Bell Jetranger, dubbed the Angel of Mercy, as operated by Peninsula Ambulance Service, the first helicopter in the world to be operated by an ambulance service. It long preceded the introduction of the first, larger Dauphin helicopter, known as AIR495, operated jointly by Ambulance Service Melbourne and Victoria Police.

9

The Work

Apprenticeship

About 80 percent of overall AO work at PAS consisted of routine patient transports for long-term chemotherapy, haemodyalysis, and other specialist treatments. At the time I began my ambulance career, only the major hospitals offered such treatments. It was common for us to transport patients to and from these hospitals twice in the course of a day shift. These trips usually required little patient treatment, other than assisting those who were nauseous and vomiting post their treatment.

Due to the distances involved to and from city hospitals, and the number of patients needing our services, we were required by our controllers to carry as many patients as possible in our AGPs. This often meant transporting one patient lying supine on the stretcher (i.e., the sickest one), seating three more on the spare stretcher with their backs to the ambulance wall, and finally a patient in the seat usually occupied by the jockey, leaving him perched and unrestrained on a steel first aid box, between the front seats: a most uncomfortable arrangement. With hindsight, we probably operated outside of Victorian road rules, but this practice carried on for many years. Other routine transports were in the local Frankston and Dandenong areas, usually for in-patients from the surrounding hospitals requiring specialist X-rays, MRIs, and blood tests.

Importantly, though, these transport cases served as an informal AO apprenticeship, where we learned how to relate to patients, particularly the elderly. We also became familiar with many of the hospital and clinic staff and learned to navigate our way around Melbourne's many medical facilities and hospitals. This included sometimes late-night transfers of patients requiring voluntary (or involuntary) admission into major psychiatric facilities, such as Larundel (now defunct). This was a large, sprawling facility made up of numerous imposing buildings from the 1940s. To arrive at night with a patient on board could be interesting, as a person appearing beside our ambulance, claiming to be from receiving staff, could just as easily have been an inmate out for an evening stroll. We made a habit of leaving our ambulance windows only partially open until we were certain.

On most weekdays, PAS patient transports began very early, carried out towards the end of nightshifts, regardless of how busy we might have been throught the night. Depending on the number and locations of patients to be picked up, one or more crews were split up from about 5 a.m. and assigned a station wagon or larger clinical bus. Pickups occurred as far south as Sorrento and Pakenham to the east. We would return about 7 a.m. to hand over our patients to the day-shift clinic transport officers (CTOs), who would complete the patients' journeys into the city for their various appointments.

One day, one of our colleagues returned from an early-morning Mornington Peninsula pickup run, carrying a jar of gleaming white almonds, given to him by one of our regular patients. She had handed over the jar, explaining that she didn't like the almonds, only their chocolate coating. I'm fairly certain that he threw them out.

10

Public Duties

■ **Days at the Races**

During the 1970s and 1980s, PAS deployed crews to public events such as AFL matches and World Series Cricket matches, both at Waverley Park Stadium (now largely demolished), and to the various steeple and flat horse racetracks located on the Mornington Peninsula. Professional jockeys would refuse to race, or even mount their rides, unless a PAS was in attendance to watch over their safety.

At the racetracks and during the course of the race program, our responsibilities included periodic checks on the jockeys in their rooms. I'm not sure any of us understood the purpose of this; apologies to them, however, as we used to get a giggle hearing them conversing, sounding as if they'd been inhaling helium. Many of them, we noted, pulled on ladies tights (presumably for warmth).

Attendance at public duty events required us to wear our peaked police-style ambulance caps. We found these to be totally impractical during operational work; however, PAS maintained that they had to be worn, especially at public duties. This was reinforced by the surprise visits of a PAS senior station officer (SSO), who would find a seat in the public stands and spy on us through binoculars. As we were always alert to them, we were rarely caught out capless. There was another risk to us being caught out, even if the SSO didn't attend: being captured by television cameras, either whilst we were driving behind the race field or attending to an injured jockey, and replayed on the nightly news programs.

Our responsibilities at race meetings began with watching the jockeys mount up in the mounting yard, then to drive our ambulance to be close but not close enough to frighten the highly strung racehorses. We then observed the horses and jockeys enter their allocated individual starting barrier. The horses were sometimes reluctant to enter such a restricted space, requiring a group of men to link arms around the horse's hindquarters and push it in to position. Occasionally, a nervous animal would buck, sending the jockey flying. When the official race starter was satisfied that the field had settled, he turned on a beacon and pressed the trigger, releasing all horses simultaneously from the starting barrier: The race was on.

We were required to follow in our AGP, along a usually sandy track just inside the perimeter of the turf racetrack. Driving on these tracks, whatever the weather, whilst trying to maintain a reasonable and consistent gap from the racing field, was both challenging and hazardous. Our AGPs were fitted with standard road tyres which easily slipped in the sand, occasionally resulting in an unexpected slide into the barrier separating us from the turf track. Should one of more zealous SSOs attend, one who had no experience of driving on sand, he might call us via his portable radio, admonishing us for staying too far behind the race group.

Once the race was under way, we followed behind, usually seeing only a cloud of grass and dust or mud, depending on the weather. Occasionally, a jockey appeared behind the cloud, sprawled out on the turf. We especially dreaded the steeplejump races, as each race meeting seemed to include at least one fall, usually due to a horse failing to completely clear one of the brush barriers. These falls often resulted in serious injuries to both jockeys and their mounts. Horses may break one or more legs and roll over or trample the dismounted jockey. Jockeys could receive head, chest, limb, and spinal injuries; however, unlike horses, they weren't as a rule put down. I treated a trampled jockey on one occasion who had a horseshoe imprint in the centre of his back.

Whenever a fall occurred, we had to work quickly to retrieve the injured jockey, as the race field may be making another circuit of the course before the race end. We would duck under the barrier, trying to keep our caps in place, and with little finesse, drag our patient under the barrier onto the safety of the sand track. The jockey's relative lack of weight and frictionless silk clothing made this action easier; despite the severity of a jockey's injuries, nothing could be allowed to halt the race. Race betting took precedence over anything else.

I attended two memorable incidents involving race horses, both occurring at the same racetrack, although some months apart. On the first occasion, we had parked our AGP near to the race barrier, ready to witness the horses and jockeys take up their positions. One of the horses, with jockey on board, walked towards our AGP. Something spooked the animal, and it reared up, throwing the jockey to the ground. He got up, uninjured; his mount, though, continued to buck wildly, its eyes filled with terror.

Suddenly, it threw its full weight aginst the left side of our AGP, which began rocking violently. I was alone in the driver's seat and momentarily lost sight of the animal before it re-appeared in the rearview mirror. At the same time, the jockey (horse, not ambulance), my colleague, and the attending SSO bolted for safety on the other side of the safety barrier. Unfortunately, my colleague, being of short stature, found himself in the path of the SSO, who picked him up and helped him over the barrier. The racehorse, meanwhile, continued to vent its rage, its hind legs kicking repeatedly at the AGP's rear doors, until it had completely kicked them in. Finally, it settled down and could be led away. In the end, only the ambulance suffered, needing to be towed away; the racehorse and humans were all unhurt.

The second occasion was very different, occurring during a flat race. Once again, we were following another cloud of dust in our AGP when a dismounted jockey suddenly appeared, standing beside the barrier rail, beating it with his riding crop. We soon saw why when we came across his mount, writhing on its back and making unearthly sounds. One of its hind legs was completely reversed, and a foreleg had been torn out, blood spurting from a severed artery with full force. A screen was placed around the poor beast, and the racecourse veterinarian quickly ended its life. The jockey was inconsolable, his mount having apparently stepped into a hole, missed during the routine track inspection. The whole scenario was pitiful, and I silently questioned the need for such suffering caused by insatiable human greed.

Amateur Scriptwriter

Whilst not strictly considered as a public duty event, PAS was occasionally requested to provide an AGP and crew to participate in the filming of television programs, commercials, and movies. Our attendance was meant to provide authenticity to the production. For AOs, these were considered plum events, removing us temporarily from routine ambulance work and being involved in the very different world of visual production. We were also happy to partake in the offerings of the production's catering truck. At the beginning of a day shift, my student AO and I were despatched to take part in the making of an Australian Broadcasting Commission (ABC) drama, titled *Spy in the Family*. We met with the director on our arrival and were advised that our role was to play an ambulance crew who had been called to transport an elderly lady from her country home. The final scene was to show our AGP driving off her property. When filming of our scene got under way, we took our stretcher into the home and loaded our patient onto it. We then made our way across lawn of the front garden. I was walking in reverse at the head end of the stretcher, looking out for obstables, and came across a trip hazard: a small tree stump that my colleague at the foot end may not spot. I mentioned this to the director, who asked, "What would you normally say to your partner?", to which I replied, "Watch out for the stump, Wayne." This was added to the script; I was chuffed.

Football, Meat Pies, and Kangaroos

We attended the Victorian Football League matches at Waverley Park Stadium during winter and World Series Cricket matches during the summer. Our role was to provide care, primarily to injured players, but extended to the public as required. We enjoyed these events, as should we be required, our job was to assess and treat and request another ambulance to attend for transport (we were never to leave the stadium during the course of a match). We were also treated to a full meal in the same dining area shared by TV commentators. I recall sitting down for our meal when a well-known TV personality, and no shrinking violet, called out, "Where's my peas?", ensuring that all that diners were aware of his presence.

Occasionally, spectator injuries occurred at the stadium, usually through falls down concrete steps, whilst concentrating on not spilling beer-filled cups. Cardiac arrests also sometimes occurred; we dreaded these, as finding the patient in a crowded stadium was difficult, and we were weighed down by our portable equipment. St John's ambulance voluntary staff also attended these events, administering first aid to the public and requesting our attendance if they deemed it warranted. One day, a crew arrived back at Frankston from the stadium, having been despatched to back up the crew on duty there to a cardiac arrest. Describing the scene, the senior AO told us that the patient was surrounded by St John volunteers, all keen to assist. His comment was apt; he said, "It was like fifteen men on a dead man's chest."

11

Shifts, Rosters, and Flag Raising

At PAS, AOs day and afternoon shifts were generally for eight, nine, or ten hours; however, they were frequently extended due to despatch to a late case or completing a long-distance transport. Night shifts of eight-hour duration began at either 11 p.m. or midnight, continuing for seven to ten consecutive shifts, concluding with a varied number of days off. Most of us sought overtime shifts to supplement our incomes.

As described previously, PAS operated a single twenty-four-hour MICA unit. The MICA roster differed completely from that of AOs, being based on the 10/14 roster, modelled on that used by the Metropolitan Fire Brigade. The roster consisted of two consecutive ten-hour day shifts, from 7 a.m. to 5 p.m., followed by two consecutive fourteen-hour night shifts, from 5 p.m. to 7 a.m. As the MICA crew were generally despatched only to time-critical cases, the 10/14 roster worked reasonably well, allowing for some rest on night shifts, although this was variable. The PAS requirement of MICA was that the crew left the Frankston headquarters at about 11 p.m. and travelled to Chelsea branch, some fifteen minutes north. Here a bedroom was set aside for the crew, much to the envy of AOs. From Chelsea, they returned to Frankston at about 6.30 a.m. to meet the oncoming day-shift crew.

Non-MICA crews on eight-hour night shifts were permitted only to "rest and recline," although we all had our own interpretations of what this meant. Although we were likely to be despatched throughout the night, we tried to nod off, upright in our mess room chairs. If all chairs were occupied, we sat on the plastic chairs in the kitchen, putting our heads on the benchtop, always alert to a zealous night-shift SSO on patrol, hoping to catch us out. To be fair, most SSOs didn't come into our mess room and would themselves try to find some sleep.

Away from the scrutiny of headquarters SSOs, night shifts at peripheral branches were more relaxed; AOs laid out blankets and pillows on floors, and a few chose to doze on AGP stretchers. At Frankston, though, regardless of how busy our nights had been, the more zealously inclined SSO would come into our mess room at about 6 a.m. and select a junior AO to raise the PAS flag in front of headquarters. The SSO would have to walk past where the flag was stored to wake us up. In protest, we would occasionally "accidentally" invert the flag on the pole, as if PAS was on a war footing. The SSOs, apart from the few who appreciated the humour, were left unimpressed and sought out the offender, who had usually left for home.

Some AOs managed to handle the effects of night shifts better than others; many of us, though, found sleep during daylight hours hard to find. Those so affected returned for the next night shift, fatigued after only a few fitful hours of sleep. Personally, as much as I found the work stimulating and challenging, I never coped well with the night shift and even later, on the MICA 14 hour night shifts, could never manage more than a few hours uninterrupted sleep.

Apart from responding to cases as required, weekends at PAS headquarters were dedicated to cleaning all emergency and clinic transport vehicles. Day-shift crews were expected to check each vehicle's equipment, wash and hand polish them, and apply "black" to all tryres. We were always dismayed if a certain SSO was rostered on the weekend, as he required us to climb up and also polish the vehicle roof.

12

Training

One of the PAS SSOs had the additional responsibility of providing initial driver training to student AOs. Curiously, this was carried out in a standard, unmarked 1.2 litre Toyota Corolla. The SSO, usually a very mild-mannered, circumspect individual, changed completely when behind the wheel. He demonstrated his high-speed driving skills by taking three students along and driving down the winding and narrow beach road between Mornington and Dromana, a distance of about seventeen kilometres. He pushed the car to its limits, leaving his passengers feeling very anxious. Each of us was then expected to drive the same road and distance, following his example. If, according to his standards,we drove too slowly, he would urge us to drive harder. The Corolla was not fitted out with with emergency beacons or a siren, and I wonder what might have transpired if we'd been stopped by police. Certainly, there was no mention of any arrangements or notification to police of our activities.

In September 1977, along with other PAS and Victorian student AOs, I was selected to attend a one week driver training course at the Goulburn Valley Driver Education Complex in Shepparton, in northeastern Victoria. There, and this time in a Ford F100 AGP, we learned advanced driving skills, including practice on a wet skid pan. Importantly, we were instructed in predictive driving (planning our drives looking well ahead of our current position on the road), something I still employ today. Under the supervision of a senior police instructor, we drove day and night, to and from Melbourne, all whilst giving a verbal narrative of our actions and potential dangers we might see ahead. We were required to use the ten minutes to 2 p.m. hands position on the steering wheel, which we had to maintain, even when turning sharp bends. I find myself often defaulting to this today.

When we had successfully completed the week's training, we were finally deemed as qualified by PAS to drive Signal 8 cases. I don't recall driving my first, although as we were well experienced by this time in driving our AGPs, driving Signal 8 did not seem a great stretch.

When driving on the Mornington Peninsula, it was not unusual to come upon four-wheel-drive vehicles towing horse floats. Horses, particularly racehorses, tend to be very skittish and may be terrified by the sound of emergency sirens. As they are confined in a very small space, with no means of escape, they react to sirens by bucking and potentially suffering injuries. Due to this, it was established practice amongst PAS crews to switch off our sirens whenever we spotted a horse float on the road ahead.

A Ford F100 AGP parked on the apron at the front of the PAS Frankston headquarters. The photo was taken in the early 1980s; the building is currently occupied by a commercial tyre outlet.

A number of AOs were assigned to each AGP, which we were expected to keep clean and restock as required (also the duty of the on-shift crew). This is Car 814, to which I was assigned; my assigned colleagues and I were proud of it, as it was one of the first of the new vehicles to arrive fitted with a single lift-up rear door. Note also the proximity of the sirens directly above the driver and jockey positions. It is not surprising that the noise of these, over time, affected our long-term hearing.

Erik Schanssema

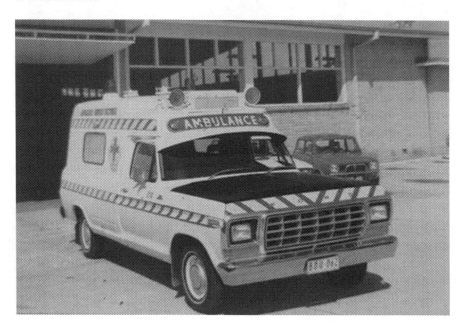

13

Rank

In order to progress through AO qualification levels, we were required to pass periodic wrirtten examinations and perform satisfactorily in scenario-based tests, using a variety of our portable equipment.

Victorian ambulance services of the time, including PAS, exhibited a somewhat paramilitary face. Student AOs progressed through a rank system from AO1 to AO2, and final full qualification as an AO3. Each new level required stitching chevrons onto our uniforms, usually lovingly done by our partners. We were extremely proud whenever we succeeded to a new level. Pictured is the PAS epaulette, indicating an AO3 qualification. We were pleased and proud to be identified specifically as PAS AOs. Below it is the early version of the ASV shoulder badge, worn across the state. In its centre is a Maltese cross, harking back to the days of the Knights of St John.

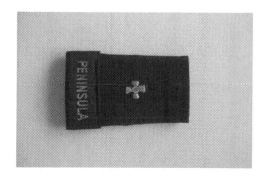

Some AOs were satisfied to plateau at the level of AO3, whilst others sought the challenge of qualifying as a training officer (TO), responsible for the training and mentoring of AO1s and AO2s. Generally, AOs progressed from AO1 to AO2 over a period of three years; a further four years' operational experience was required to become a TO. Beyond this, and having spent an appropriate and successful period of several years as a TO, an AO3 could put himself forward for MICA training, at the time the highest clinical position in Victorian ambulance services; well-qualified MICA officers could go on to become MICA TOs and MICA station officers (SOs). A relatively few AOs chose to undertake MICA; I describe later why I chose this path. Some chose instead to pursue ambulance careers in communications, becoming call taker-controllers, whilst others pursued administrative careers as SOs or SSOs.

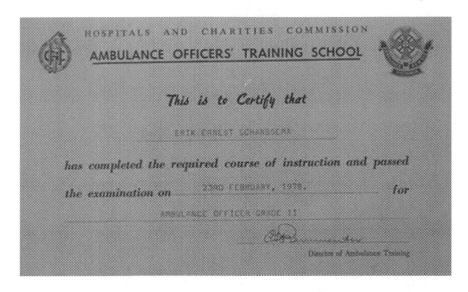

My certificate of completion, qualifying me as an Ambulance Officer Grade 2 (AO2)

14

Communication

Radios and the NATO Alphabet

Crews waiting at PAS Frankston headquarters to be despatched were called over a public address sytem by their assigned vehicle; for example, "814 for a Signal 8." On hearing this, the crew, usually whiling away the time in the mess room, would make their way to the tiny control room, where we received verbal case details through a window. We were required to record these on a notepad and repeat the details. We did the same if we received a case via radio, if we happened to be mobile. To further mitigate the chance of errors being made and provide reassurance to the controllers that our recorded details were accurate, we employed the North Atlantic Treaty Organisation (NATO) alphabet: Alpha for A, Bravo for B, and so on. Less commonly, repeating of numbers was emphasised for clarity by saying, for example, "niner" for nine. This practice faded away after a few years, mostly as it caused the majority of AOs to mock those who used it.

On arrival at a Signal 8 case location, we were required to report via radio: "814 arrived." Once we had established the nature of the case, which at times differed completely from the original case description, we were further required to provide a situation report (sitrep). This would include the number of patients and their clinical condition. Trauma patients were categorised as Alpha for minor injuries, Bravo for serious injuries, Charlie for critical injuries, and 83 for deceased patients. If backup was not already under way, we would request this at the same time, often requesting attendance of the MICA crew. Amongst ourselves, although sometimes heard over the radio, a patient's condition might be described as "82 and a half," meaning the patient was not expected to survive long.

Notorious radio "blackspots" existed in parts of PAS' operational boundaries, particularly in and around the Dandenong ranges, resulting in crews being left completely devoid of radio communication (this was before mobile phones). If a controller had not heard from a crew in a suspected or known blackspot, he might resort to sending another crew to check on the first crew's welfare. This action might assist the first crew but left the controller with two crews, now both incommunicado. Portable radios were not generally available to crews in the late 1970s. When a number of patients were spread over a large area, we had to resort to splitting up and sharing our portable equipment as best we could until backup crews arrived.

Shit, the radio button's stuck!

Crews would often complain about the nature of a case we were despatched to. We all protested if sent to what we considered a minor ailment, certainly not warranting the attendance of an emergency ambulance. Despite our complaints, we always attended whatever case was given to us, but occasionally, cases such as a patient complaining of being unable to sleep, or being hungry, tested our patience, especially during night shifts. We had to blame someone and so directed our anger at our controllers. Discussions between crew members regarding the various attributes (or as we saw it, the failings) of an individual controller occurred often when we were mobile. Unfortunately, the radio Send button often became stuck on, and this was not always immediately apparent to the crew. If between them, such an unlucky crew was maligning a controller or PAS manager, usually peppered with expletives, their conversation could be heard by every mobile ambulance crew and in the control room. More crucially, stuck radio buttons had the additional impact of halting all PAS radio communication, until it was released. Sometimes, the affected crew became aware that radio transmissions had ceased and realised what had happened. At other times, a crew could be so deep in conversation that an SSO might take a vehicle and try to locate the crew. Guilty crews were later given a severe dressing down by an SSO, but their embarassment caused the rest of us great mirth (until it happened to us, of course). No doubt, the maligned controllers felt much aggrieved.

Assault

Physical or verbal assaults on AOs, other emergency service workers, and hospital staff were common but rarely received media attention, at least in the state of Victoria. The situation has finally changed in the last few years, and legislation has been introduced to deter violent attacks on emergency service staff. Current ambulance portable and fixed radios incorporate a duress alarm which can be silently activated, alerting despatchers that a crew is at risk. In earlier days, if a crew was at risk, retreating to the ambulance was the only option.

On one occasion, my partner and I were despatched to transfer a patient from PAS Frankston headquarters through to the Alfred Hospital. The patient, as we later learned, had been seen walking down a rural road, carrying a firearm and a bottle of liquor. Police attended, and the patient apparently retreated into the rear of a home, closing a door and refusing to exit. Somehow, shooting began, and he was struck in the head by police firing through the door. The crew arrived at Frankston headquarters, where they were about to end their shift. We listened to their patient handover and greeted their escorting armed police officer, who remained seated in the front passenger seat. I was driving and tried to strike up a conversation with the police office, but he seemed only interested in watching the world go by through his side window.

My partner, Arthur, a former carpenter, was powerfully built but possessed a very gentle manner. The patient, about thirty-five years of age, also powerfully built, was lying conscious on the stretcher, with his head bandaged and an intravenous (IV) drip in place in his arm. The bullet that had struck his head had fragmented on impact, the multiple pieces lodging in his scalp, but it had apparently not pierced his skull. All was quiet for the initial part of the journey, as we made our way without lights and sirens to the Alfred Hospital, about forty-five minutes away.

The situation changed suddenly and unexpectedly as the patient, unprovoked, sat up and tore the bandages from his head and ripped out his IV line, spraying blood and IV fluid around the ambulance interior. In the rearview mirror, I could see Arthur trying to calm the patient, but this was clearly not working, as he then launched into a physical attack. Arthur was able to fend off his blows and somehow managed to restrain him. To my surprise, our escorting police officer remained completely oblivious to the noise and shouting behind him. I nudged his leg, urging him to assist Arthur, but he remained unnmoved.

By this time, we had reached the Elsternwick area, about ten minutes from our destination. Arthur was again struggling with the patient, so I picked up the radio and advised PAS control of our situation, requesting police meet us at Alfred Hospital. I spoke quietly, so as to not alert the patient and potentially exacerbate the situation. It seems he had heard me, though, as he reached picked up one of our torches and began swinging it at my head as I was driving. Arthur came to the rescue and managed to hold him off. The police officer remained unnmoved, didn't or wouldn't speak to me, and continued to look out the window. The situation was not improving, so I decided to switch on the beacons only and accelerated, avoiding the traffic by driving along the St Kilda Road tram tracks.

As I turned into the Alfred Hospital's Casualty ambulance parking bay, I passed between a gauntlet of police officers ready to assist us. I got out and opened the rear doors; the interior was liberally sprayed with blood from the patient's open IV site and his exposed head wounds. The patient had spotted the police officers and quickly mellowed, insisting though that he walk into the casualty department, wearing only his flimsy hospital gown. We escorted him into a windowless cubcle that had been set aside for us. He announced that he needed to urinate, but rather than wait, he emptied his bladder into the handwash basin. Lovely chap. He then turned to Arthur and me, declaring, "You guys are okay."

As I was cleaning up our AGP, I spoke with some of the other attending police officers; our escort had meanwhile vanished. They told me that the patient was well known to police as an alleged hitman, which in their opinion was the reason our escort did not want to get involved in assisting us, for fear of encountering the patient sometime in the future and being recognised by him. This seemed bizarre to us, but in the end, we had managed to transport the patient to his destination without further injury to him (and fortunately neither to Arthur nor myself). We bore no animosity towards our police officer. In years to come, I had many occasions to be grateful for police support and their direct intervention in several violent situations.

This case nevertheless serves to demonstrate how quickly a situation that is seemingly benign can unexpectedly turn dangerous. It also illustrates the risks under which we worked at the time, prior to the introduction of portable radios. Fortunately in this case, events took place within our ambulance, and I was able to access our fixed radio.

Playing Possum

As our experience grew, we became adept at recognising patients who we suspected were playing possum, or feigning unconsciousness. This behaviour was most commonly employed by teenagers, usually as a means of seeking attention or denying the reality of an emotional situation. To confirm our suspicions that someone was indeed conscious, we would gently brush the patient's eyelashes, which would cause his or her eyelids to move involuntarily. Another method, not strictly ethical, but used at times by our more senior, jaded colleagues, involved raising a patient's forearm over his or her face and then letting go. Patients feigning unconsciousness invariably defied gravity, as their arm always fell away from their face.

15

The patient

Assess All Ages: Unborn to Centenarians

Paramedics face each shift unaware of what it may bring. Likewise, in a single shift, patients encountered may vary in age from the unborn and newborn through to centenarians. Paramedics must be sufficiently knowledgeable and skilled at adapting their patient assessments, practices, and equipment to meet a given patient's age, medical condition, and weight (the basis for accurate drug administration calculations).

The treatment of unconscious bariatric (unusual body weight and height proportions) patients, requiring invasive airway intervention, was particularly demanding. Short, overweight patients often have short, broad necks and somewhat inflexible mandibles, making airway assessment and intubation challenging.

As practised by those working in the wider patient health care chain, AOs (and now paramedics) use the term "patient" when referring to all ill or injured persons assessed by them. The term may seem impersonal, but inherent in its use is a respect for the individual, regardless of gender, age, or background (I do not use the term "race," as in my opinion, there is only one race: the human one, to which we all belong).

AOs are human, and after years of experience, they may become jaded, particularly with case types that are seen all too frequently and are the result of self-abuse. Heroin overdoses were very common during my operational years, and a few of our colleagues referred to affected patients as "junkies" (although I did not hear the term used directly to a patient). My view was that, annoying as the frequency of these cases could be, each patient was someone's son, daughter, sister, brother, and so on.

For AOs, using the term "patient" acts also as a defensive and self-protective mechanism, allowing a degree of psychological separation from a patient's injuries and illnesses. This approach is important, as sometimes in our efforts to care for our patients, it is necessary for us to inflict pain (e.g., the insertion of an IV cannula). In the event that an AO responds to a case involving someone known to them, this protection collapses, and depending on the nature of the AO-patient relationship, it may cause the AO great distress. I describe such a case later in this book.

Assessing and treating sick and injured paediatric patients can of course be distressing, particularly in the very young, who are unable to express their sysmptoms and are often fearful of us.

Cultural Variations

Assessing patients with no (or limited) English can also be challenging, as can understanding and appreciating cultural differences. Such circumstances were frequently encountered by PAS AOs working the greater Dandeong area, where many migrants had settled. Some southeast Asian people sometimes employ *Cao Gio*, a traditional treatment used for many ailments. It involves the application of an ointment, typically tiger balm, then coins are pressed onto the skin, resulting in bruise-like circular marks (this is my understanding of the technique). One night shift, we arrived at a case, finding a male patient of Vietnamese origin, who was in a state of cardiac arrest. His torso was uncovered, and we noted the multiple raised circular impressions on his back, an unfamiliar sight to us. There was also some blood, most likely resulting from the patient falling and striking his head as he collapsed. We initiated CPR, and the MICA crew arrived shortly afterwards.

The senior MICA officer happened to notice a blood-stained meat cleaver in the kitchen, where the patient had collapsed, and immediately jumped to the conclusion that the patient had been a victim of foul play. He apparently failed to notice some nearby meat that had been cut up in preparation for a meal. As we were busy with the patient, and as he was the senior clinician at the scene, we didn't challenge him when he requested via radio the attendance of homicide police (I should point out that his actions didn't delay patient treatment). Uniformed and plainclothes police officers soon arrived and quickly surveyed the scene; they noted the absence of evidence of a possible homicide, leaving our colleague somewhat embarassed.

16

Early Experiences and Challenges

As described earlier, about 80 percent of AO operational cases involved routine patient transports, usuually for regular or specialist medical treatments. The remaining 20 percent of the work comprised a wide spectrum of emergency cases. As student AOs, it was at these cases where we were introduced to the darker, despairing aspects of life.

First Death

Prior to beginning my ambulance career, I had never seen a critically ill or injured person, certainly not a dead body. My first encounter with death followed a request from an on-scene crew for a backup crew to attend the scene of a car crash to retrieve an "83" (ambulance code for a deceased patient). My TO, Len, and I were despatched. Our task was to pick up the body and transport it to Frankston Hospital's mortuary. At the time, this responsibility fell to ambulance services, which remained the case for many more years until the Victorian Coroner's Office took over.

We arrived at the scene, noting that two cars had collided at a crossroads, obviously at high speed, in a T-bone arrangement. Nearby lay the covered body of a two-and-a-half-year-old boy, who had been thrown from his seat, through a side passenger window, and onto the roadway. Len directed me to pick him up and place him on our stretcher. Externally, other than multiple lacerations and bruising, the injuries that killed him were not evident.

I don't recall carrying him, and the whole scenario seemed surreal to me. I know I placed his body on our stretcher, ensuring he remained covered by a sheet, and wheeled him into our AGP. We left for Frankston Hospital, and little was said between us, although I recall a sense of helplessness, as this was the first patient I couldn't assist. I travelled to hospital in the front seat, acutely aware of the dead child lying directly behind me.

As I've described in chapter 7, whenever we arrived with an 83 at Frankston or Dandenong hospitals, we would advise the casualty department staff and request the mortuary key and for a doctor to examine and certify our patient. In this case, the doctor conducted his examination on our stretcher, following which we gently slid the body onto a spare stainless steel tray and again covered it with a sheet. This was my first experience of a mortuary, and I was aware of a number of other bodies laid out on trays, all with indentifying tags attached to a large toe.

Despite the fact that the patient was deceased, a full patient care record (PCR) had to be completed. This done, I left the PCR hospital copy with casualty staff but felt somehow uneasy leaving the body of this small child in a cold mortuary, in the company of other deceased hospital patients, mostly elderly. I mentioned this to Len, who being well experienced, understood and asked if I wanted to return to ensure that the body was safe. We did this, but I didn't feel in any way relieved or less disturbed.

Death never rests, and transporting 83s to hospital mortuaries was necessary around the clock. I always found entering the cold environment of a mortuary an uncomfortable experience, particularly in the early hours. Rarely were mortuaries free of bodies. I recall a night when the MICA crew had been busy attending one cardiac arrest after another, none of whom survived. We, as a non-MICA crew, were called to transport a few of MICA's patients to Frankston Hospital's mortuary. One of these transports took place around 3 a.m., and we arrived at the hospital and went through the usual processes. We had just moved the elderly deceased patient from our stretcher to an empty mortuary tray when I turned away, and my partner let out a chilling scream, followed by "He moved, he moved!" After recovering my senses, I looked back at the patient, who was most certainly deceased. My partner, however, remained convinced by what he saw (or thought he saw). As he had frightened me, I rather unsympathetically reacted by accusing him of acting like an idiot. Perhaps, though, with hindsight, his behaviour may well have been due to the number of 83s we had seen that night, or he was exhibiting signs of accumulated stress. He was an experienced AO who had begun his career as an ambulance cadet, aged only sixteen or seventeen.

For student AOs, attending and attempting resuscitations of patients in cardiorespiratory arrest, with or without MICA support, was mortifying (no pun intended). We were young and faced with providing often the last and only chance of a person's successful resuscitation. In the case of elderly patients, who were often suffering from chronic, life-threatening conditions, we were seldom successful.

In sudden, nontraumatic cardiac arrest cases, a patient's airway is frequently soiled with vomitus, requiring manual clearing, usually achieved with the suction function of the Komesaroff oxygen resuscitator. Once cleared, artificial ventilations were provided and an appropriately sized oral airway was inserted to aid the maintenance of a clear airway. The patient's nose and mouth were then sealed with the Kommy's black inflatable rubber mask, and the two-litre-capacity rubber bag, filled with 100 percent oxygen, was squeezed rhythmically, filling the patient's lungs. These actions required use of both hands and would continue until the MICA crew (where available) would attend and provide the ultimate in airway protection (intubation). This procedure requires the MICA crew to look for and sight the patient's vocal cord, then pass an endotracheal tube (ETT) past the cords, inflating its aneurysm-like cuff, ensuring its position. The ETT was then tied off around the tube external to the patient's mouth, using a length of cotton tape, and then around the neck. This achieved, only one hand was required to squeeze the bag. Observing MICA performing these advanced airway skills was fascinating for student AOs.

With a nonpumping heart in cardiac arrest, effective cardiac compressions are required until a return of spontaneous circulation (returning pulse) is achieved, until the decision is made to cease the resuscitation attempt. Placing our hands in the correct anatomical position over the patient's sternum required us to expose the patient's chest. In the frail, elderly patient, providing effective deep chest compressions frequently resulted in inadvertent fracturing of osteoporotic ribs or sternums, with often additional rib fractures occuring during the course of the resuscitation process. The breaking of ribs and sternums, felt through the heels of our hands, is disturbing, and I never became accustomed to it.

Breaking the News

As young and inexperienced student AOs, our introduction to death and grief was abrupt. Finding a means of advising partners and family members in attendance that our resuscitation efforts had ultimately failed was always difficult and stressful, especially when expressing this outcome to the elderly partner of the deceased, who may have been together for many decades. In truth, as young AOs, we could not imagine or identify with such circumstances, other than perhaps relecting on our own parents' relationship.

No formal training or guidance was provided to assist us in knowing what to say or how to say it. We either parroted the words we had heard our TOs and senior colleagues say, or we tried to find our own words suitable to the circumstances. Usually, we would try to provide some reassurance that the patient had not suffered, and how fortunate it was that his or her partner was present at the moment of death. In the circumstances of paediatric death, no words from us could possibly have assisted.

As I became familiar with death, I began to sense that something other than physical death of the body had occurred. Apart from the cessation of heartbeat and breathing and now dilated and fixed pupils (in most cases), I somehow felt that something else, nonphysical, had vacated this now-empty shell. I am not particularly religious, although I suppose I am spiritual, which again is probably defined differently by each of us. Nevertheless, it seemed to me that the deceased's spirit, life force, soul perhaps had departed. I never felt comfortable or confident enough to discuss my feelings with my colleagues during my operational years, but this was how I consistently felt throughout my career and beyond.

We all demonstrated our respect for the deceased and their families, except on one occasion (although there were no repercussions). Following yet another unsuccessful resuscitation, we were deliberating about how we would lift and return the patient's body to her bed. One of our MICA colleagues seemed frustrated by the time we were taking; he picked up the body, placed it over his shoulder, fireman-carry style, and deposited it on the bed. Job done, we thought, and no harm done; the relatives were waiting unseen in another room.

Prior to departing the home of deceased patients, we tried to leave them appearing at peace by placing the body back on their bed, closing their eyelids and mouths, finally covering the body with bedclothes; for the sake of relatives, we would leave the face exposed. Prior to this, we would remove MICA's ETT and IV lines and seal the IV sites to prevent any passive blood leakage. In preparation for moving a body, we always asked the family to move to another room. Moving a body is not a dignified process, as it sometimes emits unearthly, disturbing sounds as air is expelled from the lungs and stomach.

In cases where we learned that the deceased patient had a long medical history and was under the care of a general practitioner (GP), we were usually not required to transport the body, having contacted the GP by phone. Instead, we offered to move the body onto his or her bed, which most families desired and were appreciative of this consideration.

We always provided guidance to the newly bereaved, patiently explaining the legal requirements, including the fact that police would visit as part of that process.

The reactions of the newly bereaved varied greatly. For the most part, grief was expressed in shock or disbelief and the calling of family, friends, and sometimes neighbours. I recall an unusual reaction following our unsuccessful resuscitation of a woman only about thirty-five years of age. Her husband was considerably older, probably in his fifties, and when we advised him of his wife's outcome, asked me, "Do you know where I can get a cheap funeral?" I was taken aback and certainly didn't have a standard response that I could call on. I think that I may just have replied that he could choose an undertaker from the Yellow Pages.

Some cases had an element of humour, despite the tragic circumstances. To perform effective chest compressions in a cardiac arrest requires a hard, flat surface. Before describing the circumstances of this case, I should point out that I am in no way homophobic. My partner Rowan and I arived at a suburban home to a suspected cardiac arrest. As we pulled up, we noticed identical twin Harley-Davidson motorcycles parked side by side on the driveway. We were met at the front door by a distressed young man, who directed us to the main bedroom, the walls of which were decorated by life-sized paintings of males displaying rampant members. Above these and along the walls were pegs, from which hung many and various hats and caps from a range of occupations, reminding me of the Village People.

On the double bed lay a large, older, and nonbreathing male. We explained to his partner that we needed to move the patient to the floor to begin resuscitation. Due to the patient's weight, well over a hundred kilograms, we struggled to move him from the very soft bed. His partner suddenly commented, "He's no lightweight fairy, is he?" Somehow, we maintained our composure and just shot knowing looks at each other, no doubt responding with an appropriate reply. We commenced the resuscitation and were finally successful, the patient now having a pulse and reasonable blood pressure. The bedroom doorway and hallway were too narrow to allow us to carry the patient, spineboard, and connected equipment. As we had sufficient crews on scene, we opted instead to pass him through the low and wide bedroom window. This done, transport to hospital continued.

First Test

Again, as young, inexperienced student AOs, we were keen to demonstrate to our TOs and senior colleagues that we were coming to grips with the skills and knowledge to enable us to cope with the more challenging cases. Not surprisingly, such cases could cause us great stress and anxiety. We learnt that prehospital ambulance care does not always come with clear guidelines that deal with every situation, and a capacity to be able to adapt and innovate in rapidly changing circumstances was essential.

The first time I was seriously tested was when my partner and I were despatched to a motor car accident (MCA) at a rural crossroad, about twenty minutes from Frankston headquarters. Depending on the nature of caller descriptions, combined with the number of calls received, the PAS controller would sometimes advise us, as in this case, that it was "a bad one." I invariably found this warning to be accurate. As we were to be the first crew on scene, our tasks were to quickly assess the situation, the number of patients and their conditions, and if and what type of backup we required, including other emergency services.

This tragic chain of events began, as we later learnt, with a child apparently ingesting medication intended for his grandfather. He reacted by rushing off in the direction of Frankston Hospital in his old station wagon, taking along the child, his mother, and two other siblings. He allegedly drove at high speed through a crossroad at the same time that an empty cattle truck entered the intersection. The truck passed over the top of the station wagon, the impact removing its roof. The truck came to a stop about a hundred metres from the point of impact (see photo). I was the jockey for the shift but was not partnered with my usual TO. We arrived at a scene of total chaos and confusion, as people were dashing about and calling for our attention from numerous directions.

My attention was initially drawn to the remains of the station wagon, and I spotted a woman sitting upright on the front bench-type seat, covered in blood, but appearing conscious. Beside her lay a child, pale, bleeding, but also conscious. Another injured child lay across the rear seat. Without time to assess these patients any further, a desperate call came from the field on the other side of a barbed wire fence, someone crying out that there was a baby. I looked over and could see a small unnmoving bundle about ten metres away, attended to by one or two bystanders. I made my way towards the fence, only to be greeted by the body of the grandfather lying face-down, deep in dense blackberry vines. A quick visual and physical assessment assured me that he was dead. Reaching the child, bystanders told me that they had carried the baby from the fence, where they had found it suspended. I assessed the baby, who was about eighteen months old; he had suffered significant external trauma and was also dead. I had still not provided a sitrep but returned to the station wagon where I found the mother to have sustained serious head injuries and substantial blood loss; the child beside her and the other on the rear seat were both pale, bleeding, with altered conscious states.

I have no recollection of providing a sitrep, but assume I did, or perhaps the controller took the initiative, as I was relieved to see the MICA crew arrive. The treatment of the survivors was a blur of activity, the details of which I no longer recall. I believe that one of the children removed from the station wagon later died following transfer from Frankston Hospital to the Royal Children's Hospital. As far as I'm aware, the mother and the remaining child both survived.

I found that in a scenario such as this, determining an accurate number of patients, assessing their relative conditions, and getting treatment to the patient who most needed our intervention was extremely difficult and stressful. In such multipatient incidents, there is a risk that if we focus our attention on the first time-critical patient we encounter, we may well fail to assess or even be aware of other patients, particularly at night.

These photos of the scene described above were taken by my friend and MICA colleague Doug Quilliam, who was working in a voluntary capacity on the Langwarrin Country Fire Authority Rescue vehicle.

Different Challenges

I was still under the tutelage of a TO when, late on a wet night, we responded to suspected car-versus-pedestrian case. We arrived to find an elderly male lying immobile on the road, wearing what appeared to be a full-length World War I-style great coat. He had apparently been struck while attempting to cross a suburban road, notorious for numerous and various types of road crashes. I examined him with the aid of a torch, finding that he had suffered extensive head injuries; he was clearly deceased.

His long coat covered his lower body, and it was not until we were preparing to lift him onto our stretcher that we noticed one of his legs had been severed and was missing. Looking further up the road, we noticed a dark bundle in the middle of the road. My TO asked me to take a look, and as I approached, I picked up the whiteness of bone illuminated by a street light. The leg had been severed just below the knee, with the tibia and fibula exposed, and the foot still within its shoe.

I reported back to my TO, who simply said, "Get a towel and pick it up." It's one thing picking up an intact body, quite another picking up a severed limb. I was hesitant at first but gingerly placed a towel around it and picked it up, noting it was quite heavy, trying at the same time not to feel any self-pity.

People who had chosen suicide were another aspect of human tragedy that we became familiar with, as our experiences grew. Some choose a quick end to life, as was the case when we were despatched to a train-versus-pedestrian case. The incident had occurred as the last train for the night passed through a bayside suburb. We arrived, finding the train stopped between stations and a nearby car parked alonside the railway tracks, engine still running and headlights still on. The driver's door was left wide open. We located the body just behind the last train carriage. It appeared that the adult male patient had lain across the tracks and waited for the train. The train severed his body at the midriff, exposing his diaphragm. The lower half of his body was strewn for some distance along the tracks. His head and torso were lying face-up, and his expression did not seem to be of someone who had died peacefully. I have no recollection of removing the body parts, although this was our responsibility. Generally, we placed body parts in pillow cases. I do recall that we assessed the distressed train driver, who had spotted the man on the tracks but was unable to stop the train in time.

Crime and Paraplegia

On an April night in 1982, the female proprietor of a Mornington Peninsula pizza shop went outside to investigate a noise behind her premises. She was suddenly shot in the neck by a twenty-five-year-old male, who, as later reported in the media, held a pathological hatred for police. A responding police officer was also shot, and the hunt for the gunman got under way. It was later suggested that the gunman had also planned to ambush the first responding ambulance; fortunately, the AO responding alone had arrived on the scene from an unexpected direction. The shop proprietor had been transported for initial care and treatment to Frankston Hospital. My colleague, Tony, and I were despatched from Frankston headquarters to transfer her to the Austin Hospital spinal unit. The bullet that struck her had resulted in instant and permanent paraplegia.

As we were preparing for her transfer, police came through the casualty department doors, holding the alleged gunman up under his arms. He was unable to support himself due to a number of police bullet wounds to his lower legs, received during the manhunt. He was placed on a cubicle bed to await treatment.

We had meanwhile prepared our stretcher and transferred our patient across, ready for a slow trip to the Austin. Only an hour had passed since she had been a well woman, enjoying full mobility, now facing life in a wheelchair. As the alleged gunman was within earshot, I made certain that he could overhear our discussion with hospital staff regarding the patient's condition. It changed nothing, but I was only expressing the deep anger that I was feeling.

Human Torch

At PAS' Frankston headquarters, crews of the varying shifts often congregated to watch TV in the mess room, waiting to be despatched to the next job. One night, a group of us were watching a B-grade horror movie about a schoolgirl who was possessed by a demon; when bullied by other schoolgirls, she would grasp them, and they would spontaneously ignite. The final scene was set in the school's indoor pool, where one of the teachers sacrificed himself by seizing the girl; they both ignited and fell into the pool, which also ignited. The end.

At this moment, the controller called over the PA for my partner and me to respond to a Signal 8 case. We walked up to the control room window and were surprised when the controller informed us that we were to attend to a "human torch." For a moment, we wondered if he had been watching the same movie and this was his perverse idea of humour, but he insisted that it an actual case. We got under way and arrived at the location about fifteen minutes later. On the verge outside the address lay a large woman, smoke rising from her lower legs, where her nylon tights had been alight and had melted into her flesh.

She was barely conscious but did not seem to be in pain. Her neighbours told us that she had set herself alight within her home, which then caught fire as she ran through it, to where she lay collapsed. Rapid transport was our priority. We covered her with wet sheets, treated her with oxygen, and transported her to Frankston Hospital. She was later transferred to the Alfred Hospital burns unit but died a few weeks later, most likely due to kidney failure, common in severe burns patients. We surmised that she had probably been watching the same movie and that this had somehow triggered her actions.

Strange Fruit

Within the first few months of my operational career, I attended my first suicide. We were despatched to a location in bushland at dusk. It was cold and windy as we made our way down an unmarked path, where from a distance we were greeted by the sight of a body hanging from a large gum tree, turning in the breeze. The patient had apparently climbed high up into the tree, attached a rope, climbed to down to a lower limb, and jumped off, probably as a means of ensuring his quick demise. The body of the male patient, about seventeen years of age, was above our reach, his feet just above our heads. The fall had completely dislocated his neck, and his face appeared waxen, something I was to become familiar with in coming years.

The spectacle of his body seemed surreal, and it was difficult to imagine the distress and despair that he had suffered leading to this final act. I can still easily conjure up the scene, which repeated itself many times at the many subsequent hanging cases I attended.

Most suicide cases we attended in the late 1970s and 1980s involved hanging, most by males. Some patients, though, concocted other means to meet their demise. We found one young man in his car within a large public park. He had attached a hose from his exhaust pipe through a rear passenger window and left the car running. He was beyond resuscitation, but we also noticed a glass jar beside him on the floor, half-filled with a clear liquid; we assumed that he had also consumed this. Police arrived on scene, and one officer opened the passenger door, picked up the jar, and inhaled deeply. Fortunately, he seemed unaffected, but we gave him a gentle lecture on his folly. This was also one of the first carbon monoxide poisoning cases I had attended, which in death usually leaves the patient with a telltale pink, flushed appearance.

In my experience, and unlike many movie scenarios, most patients who commit suicide don't leave a note explaining their actions, thus leaving partners, families, and friends bewildered and forever questioning the patient's motivations. At a few of the hanging cases I attended, it seemed that the deceased person had deliberately planned the timing of their act to ensure their body would be discovered by a particular family member, including children coming home from school. In such cases, it was difficult not to feel anger towards the deceased.

Unwanted Assistance

On a warm, busy night, my new TO, Darrell, and I were despatched from Frankston headquarters to a two-car crash in Dromana, a trip of about thirty minutes with lights and sirens. We arrived to find that two sedans had struck head-on at high speed; one vehicle was on its roof. We split up, choosing a vehicle each; I went to the one overturned, torch in hand. I found the driver, a woman about thirty years of age, hanging upside down, seat belt still attached. Her face was battered and as pale as alabaster. Her long hair hung down, falling into a large pool of blood that had collected in the roof cavity—seemingly most of her blood volume. She was clearly dead.

I returned to my partner, who was busy assessing the male driver of the other vehicle. This patient was aged about thirty, unconscious, with significant head injuries and a compromised airway, filled with blood. I placed our Kommy on the ground beside the patient's head, who was partially trapped. I attached a Yankauer suction device to the Kommy and switched to the unit's suction function. Suction required the operator to place his thumb over a hole at the base of the Yankauer (often referred to as a Yanky) device, thereby closing the circuit. I leaned forward and inserted it into the patient's airway, but each time I placed my thumb over the hole, the device blew oxygen into the airway, rather than sucking it. I removed it, tried it away from the patient, and found it to be working perfectly. I tried once more; again the device blew. I then heard Darrell call out, "Hey, get your hand off that!" He had spotted a bystander, probably thinking that he was assisting us, close off the suction at the Kommy's source each time I turned away to use the Yanky sucker.

The MICA crew arrived soon after and intubated the patient, as his airway continued to be obstructed due to uncontrolled bleeding. Police arrived also and may have had some prior knowledge of the male patient, as they went straight to the vehicle's trunk and lifted out a loaded rifle. It was their belief that he was on his way to confront his ex-partner, who lived further south on Mornington Peninsula. Instead, an innocent woman was killed.

▮ Lucky Escape

To ensure that PAS resources were available in all regions of its operational area, controllers frequently moved crews around like chess pieces. This was common at Frankston headquarters; crews were often despatched towards the Dandenong area, where local crews were depleted. Sometimes, crews were required to cover both the Frankston and Dandenong areas when both were short of available crews. In such cases, a crew would be despatched to the Thompson Road branch, a fictional location, actually referring to an intersection roughly midway between Frankston and Dandenong. Here they would wait, sometimes an hour or more, bored, waiting on their next directive. If a crew had been waiting there an extended time, feeling abandoned, they might remind the controller via radio saying, "814 *still* at Thompson Road branch."

One night, again working with Darrell, we were moved from Frankston to cover the Chelsea area. We weren't long at the Chelsea branch before being despatched to back up the MICA crew at a single-vehicle crash some distance south of Frankston. It was late, and the roads were wet. We arrived about thirty minutes later; approaching the scene, we noted the usual multiple flashing beacons of other emergency vehicles. Police had also ignited violet flares, set up at intervals on the approach to the incident scene. At first, we did not see the wrecked vehicle, but we noticed the MICA vehicle parked on a 45 degree angle on the edge of the road. I decided to park parallel to MICA, on the near side, on the incident approach side.

We got out and found the MICA crew busy with their patient, the sole occupant of a high-speed sports car that had evidently slid off the wet road surface, into a deep ditch beside the road; fortunately, it had remained upright. The patient was unconscious, and to assist in keeping her airway clear, the MICA crew asked me to support her head. This required me to position myself behind her and perch on what remained of the roof (see photo).

As I lifted her jaw, I noticed that her forehead had been deformed, and brain matter was evident (no airbags at this time). This was another unwanted first: seeing brain matter, particularly in a patient still alive. I tried to hold her skull together and maintain a reasonably clear airway as the MICA crew prepared to lift her from the vehicle. This achieved, we wheeled her into the MICA vehicle. The MICA crew required ongoing assistance, so I sat beside the patient, behind the jockey seat, still maintaining a clear airway. The MICA vehicle's rear door remained open, and I suddenly saw Darrell, running past the rear of the vehicle, yelling, "Shiiiiit!" At the same time, I heard the sound of tyres skidding on the wet road, approaching rapidly. It ended with a loud crash, and looking through the small window beside me, I saw our AGP sliding sideways towards us, stopping just short of the MICA vehicle.

A car driver, who had apparently been drinking, was surprised to come upon the police flares; he braked hard and lost control. As far as I was aware, he was uninjured, but our AGP was damaged where it had been struck hard below the patient transport compartment. Had I not parked our AGP on MICA's near side, the vehicle would have struck where I was seated.

The patient was taken in critical condition to the Royal Melbourne Hospital (RMH); however, I'm unaware of her final outcome. Following the case and during our cleanup, I was disturbed to find brain matter had stained my jacket sleeve.

How to Rustproof an Ambulance

On a busy weekday, my colleague, Doug Quilliam, and I were despatched to Frankston Hospital Casualty Department for the urgent transfer of a young boy, who was deteriorating following his diagnosis of epiglottitis (an inflammatory condition causing the airway to narrow; the relative size of a child's airway may lead to rapid airway closure), to the Royal Children's Hospital (RCH). Doug and I were not MICA qualified at the time, and Frankston Hospital had sent a doctor to escort the patient, in case he required intubation.

I travelled in the rear with the patient and doctor, providing assistance as required. Doug drove under Signal 8 conditions, and the journey was progressing smoothly until we came to the intersection of Swanston and Flinders Street in Melbourne. Traffic was still permitted along Swanston Street at this time, and during daylight hours, it was usually busy. Doug decided to travel up the tram tracks that lie in the centre of Swanston Street, normally restricted to trams only, but also accessed by emergency services. As we passed St Paul's Cathedral on our right, I looked up and noticed that we were quickly approaching a long section of freshly laid concrete, within which the tram tracks are laid.

The doctor also looked up, saw what was about to occur, and turned to me, asking, "He's not going to, is he?"

It was a rhetorical question. as it turned out; before I could answer, we were driving through the concrete, audibly spattering the underside of our AGP. This continued for a lengthy period, and as I looked up again, I saw a man resembling Mario (from the video game) performing star jumps and waving his trowel. Doug remained focussed, and we literally ploughed on through; the fresh concrete ended at about the Lonsdale Street intersection. Within a few minutes, we arrived safely, although somewhat heavier, at the RCH. Should he have done it? Of course.

On our return trip, we decided it would be circumspect to take another route around the city. We later heard that our ASM colleagues were blamed for our efforts, although we didn't escape the wrath of the PAS chief mechanic when we arrived back at Frankston headquarters. The concrete had set hard by this time, sealing the underside of the AGP.

Unexpected Encounter

Apart from our regular clinic transport patients, the vast majority of our patients were strangers to us, who we met often in their time of need. As many PAS AOs also lived on the Mornington Peninsula, there was always a risk that we might be responding to a family member or friend, something we dreaded. Late one night, David Cooper (see Foreword) and I responded to a two-car head-on crash. We arrived, finding two identical Datsun 180b sedans had struck at high speed, headlight to headlight. Each was carrying just the driver. We chose a car each, and as I approached the driver's window, the female driver asked, "Erik?" She had multiple facial lacerations, caused when her head had struck the steering wheel and windscreen. At first, I didn't recognise her. She was able to give me her name, and I realised that she was a local police officer, well known to me and many of my colleagues. I reassured her that we would look after her, but then I looked into the remaining space between her and the vehicle dash. On impact, both her femurs had punched through her knees, leaving them completely exposed. Fortunately, she was in a position that restricted her view. I didn't tell her what I could see, just that we would get her out and off to hospital soon.

I met up with David, whose male patient was suffering from very similar injuries. We planned how we would extricate our patients, and as our AGP was fitted with two beds, we could transport both. We treated our patients with pain relief and oxygen, and we covered the exposed bones with clean sheets, onto which we poured some sterile water to prevent the bones from drying out. We loaded and transported them in a way that kept them from seeing their injuries. Arriving in Frankston Hospital's Casualty Department, staff were silent and recoiled as we lifted the sheets to show the patients' injuries. In the process of writing this book, David reminded me that an on-call orthpaedic surgeon arrived and, on uncovering my patient's sheet, collapsed onto her bed.

A year or two later, I happened to come across my former patient at Frankston Hospital, where she was undergoing ongoing rehabilitation. I was pleased to see that despite having to walk aided by two sticks, she was making progress.

Recalling this case reminded me that we could never know who our next patient might be. It was also a reminder of the types of injuries we saw prior to the introduction of vehicle airbags; even though wearing seat belts was compulsory, not everyone complied (in the case described above, seat belts were worn by both patients).

Needles and Spoons

Heroin abuse was already a well-established social problem in Melbourne when I began my ambulance career in 1977. Heroin overdoses occurred across suburban Melbourne, although incidents were concentrated in St Kilda and Footscray, as was crime perpetrated by addicts. The incidents of heroin overdose was also increasing in the Frankston and Dandenong areas.

As an opiate, heroin has a rapid respiratory depressive effect; overdoses often result in unconsciousness and respiratory arrest, which if left untreated, result in death. As a student AO, illicit drug use and its consequences were foreign to me, although frequent exposure would lead me to think of heroin overdoses, in particular, as just another job.

Most heroin overdose cases involved patients in their twenties, although we would occasionally find a patient in his or her forties. Patients who had overdosed on heroin usually presented to us as unconscious, nonbreathing, and blue. In the late 1970s, only MICA carried and administered Naloxone (generic name: Narcan), a highly effective opiate antagonist. Where MICA was unavailable, we would treat the patient with supportive ventilation with the Kommy's bag and mask, providing 100 percent oxygen. If the patient had overdosed shortly before our arrival, this treatment sometimes resulted in the patient's own respirations recommencing, followed by a return to consciousness.

Where MICA did attend and time was on the patient's side, intravenous or intramuscular Narcan, supported by oxygen therapy, was usually effective within a minute or two. A patient who had been unconscious, nonbreathing, and blue would suddenly sit up and immediately want to abscond. Many feared that we would call the police, but unless the patient became violent, we never did (police were not interested in responding to what were essentially medical cases).

We always offered to transport resuscitated heroin overdose patients to hospital; invariably, this was rejected. We would leave the patient with appropriate instructions and, where available, also instruct a non-drug-affected friend to call 000 should the patient become unconscious again. Some overdose patients we were unable to resuscitate, due to the length of time that they had been nonbreathing; their bodies were often in a state of rigor mortis. These cases usually resulted from individuals shooting up alone and only being discovered when it was too late. There was a public myth that patients resuscitated from heroin overdose would become violent, as we had spoilt their hit. This was not my experience in the more than one hundred cases I attended, both as an AO and later as a MICA officer. In fact, many resuscitated patients expressed their gratitude, being fully aware that their lives had just been saved. Rather, in my experience, patients affected by alcohol were far more likely to be violent and unpredicatable in their behaviour. I attended many heroin overdose cases where the patient was deceased, having collapsed wherever they had decided to inject, sometimes with a needle still in an arm. Whether they were first-time users or established addicts was not always clear; some, though, did exhibit the so-called track marks. When some addicts could not find an arm vein as a result of frequent injections, they might resort to injecting in unlikely places, such as between their toes.

We were soon aware if a new batch of heroin hit the streets, as it would soon be followed by a spate of overdoses. Cases of multiple heroin overdoses at the same location also happened from time to time. I recall responding to an apartment where we found four unconscious overdosed patients. Fortunately, we were backed up by the MICA crew. In addition to our Kommy, we carried a separate resuscitation bag and mask, with which we could provide assisted ventilations, vital in such situations, where we had just enough equipment for the four of us to treat the four patients; they were all successfully resuscitated.

Rarely did we find heroin in its powdered form at overdose scenes; usually, we would find only pieces of aluminium foil, mini rubber balloons, spoons, and the inevitable needles, sometimes containing liquid. On some occasions, we arrived at a suspected heroin overdose to find one or both parents unconscious and their children wandering about amongst drug paraphernalia. In situations such as this, even if we managed successful resuscitations, we would request police attendance, only for the sake of the children's welfare. We would not leave the scene until they arrived.

One very cold typical Melbourne winter day, we responded to a suspected heroin overdose on the rooftop car park of a suburban shopping centre. There we found a single vehicle with two adults lying unconscious outside the vehicle and a two-year-old child watching from his rear car seat. Sadly, we were only successful in reviving the child's father. Police attended and took over the child's welfare.

During the early 1980s, with the rising spectre of HIV and AIDS, we received a warning that a few criminally minded drug addicts were setting so-called "mantraps" for unsuspecting emergency service workers attending overdose cases. The motivation of these individuals was unclear, and whether directed at police, AOs, or both, we didn't know. Thin disposable rubber gloves of course offered no protection from sharp needles, and we became very cautious whenever handling unconscious overdose patients.

My only encounter with what might have been a mantrap occurred when we found an unconscious nonbreathing male lying on a bed, on his back. To resuscitate him effectively required us moving him onto the firm base of the floor. As I put my gloved hands under his back, I spotted a syringe with a needle still attached. This was most unusual, as we would normally find the needle and syringe lying beside the patient or nearby. I was fortunate not to receive a needle-stick injury.

Heroin addicts were known to favour particular locations for shooting up. We became familiar with most of these, particularly around the Frankston, Dandenong, and Springvale areas. Examples of locations included under railway bridges, shopping strip rear alleys, and derelict houses. We were despatched to a suspected overdose at such a house. We carried our portable gear in, finding the front door wide open, and a very large collection of spent needles and syringes throughout all the rooms. In a bedroom at the rear of the property, we came across an unconscious, young male patient, alone and with very shallow respirations. He lay surrounded by needles, making it completelty unsafe for us to kneel beside him. Instead, for our own safety, we dragged him to a relatively clear area and managed to resuscitate him. He was conscious within a few minutes, and we gave him our standard lecture, reminding him how close he had been to death. He followed the usual script by refusing our offer of transport to hospital.

Familiar Places

For the most part and for most people, revisiting places from their past arouses pleasant, nostalgic memories. For AOs, driving past a location where we had attended a past traumatic event may trigger entirely different emotions. For me, there is a section of a usually busy suburban road that I will always try to avoid. Within only about a hundred-metre section of this road, there is a public swimming pool, a railway crossing, and a bridge over a drainage canal. Along this section, over just a few years, I attended a series of traumatic cases, including the deaths of two brothers, killed when their car rolled over, leaving one of them resembling a wrung-out dish cloth. Nearby, I attended to a pedestrian killed by a car, resulting in his leg being severed (as described earlier), a woman who had been viciously assaulted, resulting in a severed artery spurting from her scalp, a teenager found drowned under the pool cover of the public swimming pool, and a pedestrian struck and killed by a train at the railway crossing. I should note that these were just the cases attended by me and my colleagues at the time, along this section of road.

Similarly, a several-kilometre-long stretch of highway was notorious for high-speed vehicle crashes, often head-on, also often resulting in multiple time-critical and dead patients. I attended a most unusual case along this road following the crash of a medium-sized truck that had run into the rear of a similar sized truck, the impact causing the truck in front to roll off the road. We found the driver of this vehicle lying dead nearby. His truck was upright, and looking in for possible passengers, we noticed that his seat belt remained buckled up: a freakish sight. We supposed that the impact had thrown the driver backwards and out through a small window behind the driver's seat as the truck rolled.

Disgust and Tragedy

Late one night, we were despatched to a local suburban police station to assess a child; no other information was given. We arrived and were taken to an interview room, where a young male child, about two years of age, was standing on a low table, for reasons unknown. The first sight of him remains deeply imprinted. He was very quiet, not crying, just gazing blankly. He was wearing shorts under which a trail of dried blood had run down one leg. We immediately suspected the worst. The patient was accompanied by a close male relative, who had told police that the child had apparently left his bedroom and wandered out onto the street, where he had been assaulted. The relative, who seemed very calm, had taken him to the police station.

As the patient was not actively bleeding and did not appear distressed, we thought it best not to examine him further. We transported him and the relative, accompanied by a police detective, who intimated to me, out of the relative's earshot, his suspicions regarding the perpetrator. We arrived at the Royal Children's Hospital with the patient's condition unchanged. I do not need to expand on our emotions regarding this awful and sad case.

Patient Treatment Limitations

In brief, MICA was initiated in the early 1970s, primarily as a means of providing on-scene treatment of patients suffering from suspected acute myocardial infarctions (AMIs), or in lay terms, heart attacks. Heart muscle tissue, injured or infarcted (dead), may be complicated by arrythmias, sometimes lethal, such as ventricular fibrillation (VF). Prior to the introduction of MICA, many patients suffering AMIs and arrythmias did not survive. Equally important, it was hoped that the early treatment of suspected AMI patients would improve patient outcomes by reducing further loss of myocardial tissue and preventing arrythmias. Melbourne's first MICA unit (based on a similar Belfast model) was trialled at the Royal Melbourne Hospital. The crew was made up of two senior AOs, who had undergone advanced training, and an RMH doctor. It soon became evident to the accompanying doctors that the AOs, with their enhanced knowledge, skills, equipment, and drugs, could effectively provide the same treatment as the doctor, who could return to working in the hospital environment. The MICA system quickly established its success in improving patient outcomes, and it was recognised that MICA crews could potentially improve the outcomes of patients suffering from non-cardiac events, such as those involved in significant trauma, diabetic coma, and compromised airways. A second Melbourne MICA unit was soon after established at PAS. The full history of MICA and its continual and evolving development, including the establishment of MICA flight paramedics, remains to be written.

As described earlier, across the entirety of PAS' operational areas, only a single MICA unit was available until the amalgamation of ASM and PAS (becoming MAS) in 1989. Until that time, if more than one critical event occured within PAS' boundaries, crews frequently were left to rely on their AO skills, their knowledge, and their more limited equipment. Effective airway management is critical in patients suffering acute respiratory distress, such as asthma and acute pulmonary oedema (APO). Some of these patients required urgent intubation. Where MICA was unavailable, AO crews were limited to providing oxygen therapy via mask, and in the case of APO patients, intermittent positive pressure ventilations (IPPVs), using the Kommy's inflatable mask. This treatment in patients who were still conscious was often distressing for them (and AOs), as they frequently sensed that the pressure of the mask was further restricting their respiratory efforts. These patients were often deteriorating rapidly, urgently requiring intubation, both to improve their respiratory status and to allow their exhausted bodies a reprieve from their struggles. If MICA were available to intervene with such critically ill patients, they could also potentially improve patient outcome through use of the appropriate drug.

I experienced the frustration of being in situations where as an AO, I knew what further urgent treatment my patients required, but I was limited by my non-MICA skills and equipment. Due to being exposed to many such cases, I strongly desired to achieve MICA qualification. In the intervening years, there was much to experience and learn.

17

MICA Ambulance Crash

Very early in my career, having only just been promoted from student AO to an AO1, I arrived for a day shift at Frankston headquarters to find that my partner for the day had called in sick. I reported to the day-shift SSO, who directed me to do some menial tasks. After a time, he called me over, telling me that I was required to assist the MICA crew who were on scene with a patient they had resuscitated at an Aspendale public golf course. The SSO drove me to the scene, and we arrived to find the MICA crew in the process of loading their unconscious patient into the back of their vehicle. The patient had been intubated but remained nonbreathing. My task was to provide ventilations via the Kommy's black bag, squeezing it every four to five seconds, using about a quarter of the bag's capacity, not stopping until the patient was connected to a hospital ventilator.

I took up my position beside the patient's head and behind the front passenger seat. The MICA officer driving switched on the lights and sirens, and we headed along Nepean Highway towards Frankston Hospital. The patient's condition remained unchanged, and we had only been travelling for a few minutes when I heard our driver unleash a loud expletive. This was followed by screeching tyres and the sound of rending metal. From this moment, events occurred in slow motion. First, I noticed my MICA colleague who was seated farther to the rear of the vehicle suddenly levitate from his seat and begin to move to my left. At the same time, items such as scissors, forceps, and other equipment normally hanging from hooks attached to a board opposite me also took flight. I then realised I was also in flight, albeit briefly, as I collided with the passenger seat back rest, ending up in the footwell. I probably suffered a brief period of altered consciousness, as the next thing I recall was seeing the patient's face next to mine in the footwell. I saw that his endotracheal tube had been dislodged, and I instictively pushed it back into his airway.

As I later learnt, we had struck a small car that, despite our lights and sirens, had turned from a side street, directly into our path. The MICA vehicle struck the car just behind the driver's seat, fortunately saving the driver from injury. My recollections of what happened next are fragmentary, although I'm fairly certain that I reached for the radio microphone dangling above and reported that we had crashed and needed assistance, but when asked our location, I had no idea. Apparently, no crews were available to come to our aid, but one of the controllers calculated where he thought we could be and headed towards us in a spare AGP.

The force of the impact, despite the patient having been restrained on MICA's stretcher, had flung him forward, his head striking the upright metal bar which normally held the stretcher in place. It tore his scalp open, resulting in copious blood loss.

The MICA stretcher was a bespoke item designed only for the MICA-configured ambulance and could not be locked into the stretcher floor rails of a standard AGP. With the controller's arrival in a spare AGP and with the MICA vehicle out of action, we would have to find a way to complete the patient's journey to hospital. We removed the AGP's main stretcher and replaced it with MICA's plus the patient. We held the stretcher in place manually until we reached Frankston Hospital. Despite the patient's additional trauma and significant blood loss, his condition somehow remained unchanged, requiring only ongoing supported ventilations. I vaguely recall holding the stretcher in place.

At the casualty department, I was only aware of a sharp pain in my hip; otherwise, I seemed okay. Happily, despite both his cardiac arrest episode and our crash, the patient made a complete recovery. My MICA colleague who had been in the rear of the MICA vehicle with me seemed to be behaving erratically, but our MICA driver was unhurt. All three of us returned for our shifts the following day, when clearly we should not have, especially as the two of us who had been with the patient had both suffered concussion.

On the same day, I was called into the SSO's office, who pushed an insurance claim form before me, saying that I was required to sign it, as the driver of the ambulance. He did not ask me any questions regarding my wellbeing or indicate any appreciation for me returning to work immediately after the crash. His demeanour seemed out of character, as my previous interactions with him had left me with an impression of a caring individual. Many thoughts went through my mind, including any potential implications for my ongoing employment should I refuse to sign. As in a line from a bad movie script, he said, "If you don't sign it, we'll make it look like you did."

At this point, I just stood up and left his office without saying anything further (and without signing the form), waiting on whatever the consequences might be. I discussed what had just transpired with the MICA crew, who believed that PAS was trying to protect itself from insurance implications, as in their view, both MICA crew should have been in the rear, treating the patient, leaving me to drive. If this was the case, I would dispute this, as assisting MICA in such cases broadened our experiences, without risk to the patient. In any case, I heard nothing further from management and did not see the completed claim form again.

Following the patient's recovery, the MICA crew reunited with him and were each given several new body shirts (all the rage at the time). As the junior AO, I received nothing; I guess I had to appreciate the humour.

The photo below shows the interior of the PAS MICA vehicle as it was configured at the time of the crash. The stretcher has been temporarily removed for cleaning. Although not shown clearly, the board from which various implements hang for ready access is attached to the right wall. The bar that holds the stretcher in place and on which the patient was injured is visible in the bottom centre. Once I achieved my MICA qualification, I worked in this vehicle between 1984 and 1989. Note the single fixed radio above and between the front seats and the Lifepak 5 cardiac/monitor defibrillator fitted on top of the frame behind the driver's seat. The Lifepak 5 was favoured over future models by many MICA officers; one senior MICA officer insisted that patients jumped higher during defibrillation, as opposed to other machines (I'm still not sure if he was serious). The PAS MICA also carried a twelve-lead electrocardiogram (ECG), innovative for the time.

18

Mobile Intensive Care Ambulance

During the 1970s and 1980s, the MICA concept continued to develop, with increasing patient treatment protocols and drugs. Updates to MICA practices were frequent; training was conducted in lecture settings twice a year. MICA's value in improving patient outcomes in a prehospital setting was receiving recognintion by the wider medical community. Victorian government funding limitations allowed for only a limited number of MICA units, distributed across the state. Due to this restriction and despite the scale of PAS' operational area, PAS continued to operate only one unit. At times, PAS experimented with providing MICA paramedics who were on the reserve roster with the key MICA equipment. This proved successful, although the crew also responded to non-MICA cases, thereby limiting their availability.

At PAS, gaining selection for the one or two MICA positions that became available annually (although inconsistently) was highly competitive, although relatively few AOs aspired to it. Prospective MICA applicants were required to demonstrate consistency in providing high-quality patient care, produce well-documented patient care records (PCRs), and successfully fulfill the role of training officer (TO) for a number of years. Ensuring twenty-four-hour, 365-day-a-year coverage required a minimun of fifteen MICA officers to fill the 10/14 roster, this number accounting also for those on leave or out sick.

The MICA roster was divided into four lines, designated A, B, C, and D; there were two MICA officers per line. To gain experience and as part of the qualification process, MICA students were rostered with a MICA TO for two periods of eight weeks. As a consequence, some "permanent" MICA officers were required to step off the MICA roster for periods and undertake a stint on reserve and crew-up with an AO. This arrangement had the unintended advantage of resting MICA officers by returning them to general AO ambulance work (responding to cases that were not critical).

To be considered for MICA training selection at PAS usually meant a wait of seven years from commencement as a student AO. Most of us believed this was appropriate, allowing us time and experience to improve our practices and knowledge. In 1984, in my seventh year at PAS, I felt I was ready and sufficiently experienced to put myself forward for selection. Four of us were selected, though this was reduced to two: Doug Quilliam and me. Prior to progressing further, we were required to attend a week of intensive study and testing at East Melbourne, known as Phase 1. Our qualified MICA colleagues had told us of their experiences during this week, reminding us how tough it was and that not all would succeed.

My passion for MICA was well known amongst my PAS colleagues, and I was both proud and embarassed to make the front cover of our in-house satirical magazine, *Pointy Head*. I was depicted holding a voodoo doll, sticking pins into the names of other prospective MICA candidates.

MICA was sometimes irreverently referred to as the Frog Squad, so called as many of MICA's patients "croaked." This actually reflected the fact that MICA frequently attended elderly patients in cardiac arrest, most of whom were either deceased on arrival or could not be resuscitated. It followed then that MICA students were referred to as "Tadpoles."

Phase 1

Phase 1 was conducted from Monday to Friday at the Ambulance Officers Training Centre (AOTC) in East Melbourne. We prepared ourselves with a good deal of prestudy, in the knowledge that course failure excluded us from progressing further. The lectures included in-depth study of anatomy, physiology, cardiology, pharmacology, and etiology, all with copious quantities of handouts. Each night, following lectures, we studied the day's notes and handouts. In addition to this, we were expected to study and learn verbatim two or three MICA protocols and associated drug description sheets. The following morning, our knowledge would be tested, accumulating as the week progressed. By Friday, it was expected that we could recite each one, verbatim.

As the pressure increased, we studied late into the night and early each morning, before the lectures. By Wednesday, one or two participants succumbed to the pressure and dropped out, returning to their respective ambulance service. No shame was attached to those who could not continue; each one of us at some point during the week contemplated following their example. Those remaining pushed on, absorbing the building pressure as Friday loomed.

As individuals, we experienced and coped with the pressure in varying ways. To illustrate, one of our colleagues was studying late at night when he picked up two alcohol swabs (used in preparing an IV or IM site) and pushed one up each nostril. Strangely, at the time, this didn't seem odd at all. I have little recollection of the Friday examinations but somehow got through.

In hindsight, the psychological stresses associated with Phase 1, combined with minimal sleep, was in many ways unnecessary, unproductive, and potentially damaging. We supposed that the concept was to test our potential for dealing with the pressure of managing actual MICA cases.

Below are examples of a MICA drug description sheet and a MICA protocol taken from the total of twenty-five drugs and twenty-nine protocols listed in the 1985 *MICA Drugs and Protocols* handbook. We were required to maintain a verbatim knowledge of the entire book (referring to the handbook in an urgent situation in the field was not always practical).

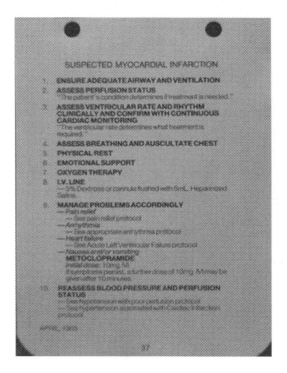

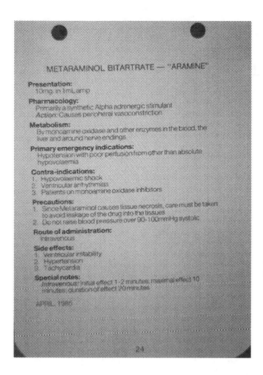

METARAMINOL BITARTRATE — "ARAMINE"

Presentation:
10mg. in 1mL amp

Pharmacology:
Primarily a synthetic Alpha adrenergic stimulant
Action: Causes peripheral vasoconstriction

Metabolism:
By monoamine oxidase and other enzymes in the blood, the liver and around nerve endings.

Primary emergency indications:
Hypotension with poor perfusion from other than absolute hypovolaemia

Contra-indications:
1. Hypovolaemic shock
2. Ventricular arrhythmias
3. Patients on monoamine oxidase inhibitors

Precautions:
1. Since Metaraminol causes tissue necrosis, care must be taken to avoid leakage of the drug into the tissues
2. Do not raise blood pressure over 90-100mmHg systolic

Route of administration:
Intravenous

Side effects:
1. Ventricular irritability
2. Hypertension
3. Tachycardia

Special notes:
Intravenous: Initial effect 1-2 minutes, maximal effect 10 minutes, duration of effect 20 minutes

APRIL 1985

24

The Course Proper

Having successfully passed Phase 1, we moved on to the full and no-less-intense full MICA course. Six months of lectures, study, and practical examinations followed, including a two-week coronary care course at the Royal Melbourne Hospital (RMH), shared with nurses aspiring to qualify for coronary care. During our time at RMH, we arrived very early, prior to the start of formal lectures, and at the end of the day, we continued to study late into the night. All MICA students passed this course, following which we were presented with an RMH Coronary Care certificate; this was considered to be our MICA practising certificate.

Belen, pregnant at the time with our son, Julian, was wonderful and always prepared to assist me with my studies at home.

Throughout the MICA course, we were mentored by Cheryl Wilkinson-Cooper, a senior AOTC lecturer. Cheryl's encouragement and belief in us greatly aided us in coping and getting through the course. Cheryl and her husband, Greg (also MICA qualified), remain great friends to this day. Each morning, Cheryl tested us on our MICA drugs and protocols knowledge, which we were all trying to commit to memory. I'd become a little anal, as I was usually able to recite the relevant page number; Cheryl would often turn to me, expecting me to repeat it.

Returning to the AOTC and as part of our training, we practised inserting IV lines into quite realistic training arms, which included "working" veins. We also practised taking each other's blood. I practised on my good friend Doug (infamous for taking our AGP through fresh concrete on Swanston Street). I was clearly hesistant, so Cheryl said I should go deeper. I did, but Doug crumpled at the knees.

Under the guidance of Dr Frank Archer (AOTC senior lecturer), and to aid us in better understanding human airway anatomy, we examined lamb airways, with lungs still attached. This was unpleasant and not necessarily analogous to human anatomy; it nevertheless served to instruct.

We learned that if a patient's lung had been lacerated in significant chest trauma (e.g., pierced by a fractured rib or in a stabbing), this may lead to lung collapse, resulting in air being trapped within the pleural cavity. Left untreated and with the air pressure increasing, the patient's condition may rapidly deteriorate, compromising the heart's pumping capacity, perhaps leading to death. We learned how to recognise this syndrome, known as a tension pneumothorax (TPT), and how to relieve it via emergency chest decompression. To do this required performing an initial test for air in the pleural space by inserting a fine-gauge needle, which, if the test is positive, is replaced by a much larger needle attached to a one-way valve, allowing air to escape and no longer accumulate in the pleural space. Successful decompression of a TPT (as an isolated condition) leads to rapid patient improvement and may be life-saving.

The successful decompression of a TPT requires prompt recognition, assessment, and very accurate placement of the needle between specific upper ribs. Inaccurate placement may result in failure to achieve decompression or inadvertent blood vessel laceration.

In the lecture room, we practised locating and marking the correct anatomical location for needle insertion on each other's chests. As this was a new and important life-saving skill, and to prepare us for actual in-field TPT cases, we travelled to the Coroner's Office complex in South Melbourne. Here, we were presented with the body of a male in his forties, whose chest had been uncovered. The circumstances of his death were not explained to us, although he appeared uninjured. He lay on a metal tray in an area, separated from other bodies pending autopsy. I found this scenario disturbing; there was complete silence amongst our training group.

The object of this training was twofold. Firstly, we were each required to demonstrate that we employed a systematic approach to identifying the correct anatomical position. Secondly, we were to appreciate the sensation of actual penetration of both small and large needles through a patient's skin and muscle and into the chest cavity. We each successfully carried out our task. I felt quite disturbed during my turn and can still recall the feel of the needle as it passed through each anatomical layer. I found that when I decompressed a TPT for the first time on a car crash victim, the sensation matched my experience at the Coroner's Office, and the decompression was successful.

Prospective Coronary Care nurses and MICA students of the 1984 Royal Melbourne Hospital Coronary Care course. Much to my shame, I am responsible for the rabbit fingers above a colleague's head. I blame the stress of the course.

The all-male MICA students, left to right: Ken Bailey, Doug Quilliam, Gary Becker, myself, Greg Savage, John Fahey, and Alan Close. Second from the left is Cheryl Wilkinson-Cooper, our friend and mentor thoughout the MICA course.

New Skills

Effective and appropriate airway management is a critical MICA skill, as is making the correct clinical decisions appropriate to the circumstances of a patient's health crisis. We learned to be adept at assessing the airways of newborns through to adults.

Paediatric airways are, of course, relatively small compared to adults. Congenital airway disorders in paediatric cases can be very challenging, particularly if intubation is required. To prepare us, MICA training included a day in theatre with an anaesthetist at the Royal Children's Hospital. Depending on the day's case list and type, we practised inserting IV lines and inserting endotracheal tubes. This session was invaluable, as once we were out in the field, we were on our own when managing airways in critically ill paediatric patients. Later in my MICA career, I seemed to attract cases involving very sick or injured children, particularly during my time at the MICA 7 unit at Dandenong. Our MICA training also included a day in theatre with an anaesthestist, inserting IV lines and intubating adult cases. Sometimes, if the anaesthetist (always male in my experience) was confident in our skills and once the patient was intubated, he might leave us to ventilate the patient whilst he left the theatre to make calls.

Airway management in the field is completely different from the environs of a steril, well-lit operating theatre, where patients arrive with a clean airway and having fasted, preventing the chance of passive vomiting. Anaesthetists also have the advantage of having the patient in theatre at the optimum height for intubation. The majority of in-field MICA intubations are carried out at ground level or where the patient is in situ (e.g., trapped in vehicle wreckage). Lighting was of course variable, depending on location and time of day. Patients requiring intubation most frequently have airways soiled by vomitus or blood. Patient's body proportions and weight are also a factor (e.g., patients with a so-called "bull" neck can be challenging to intubate). Intubating a patient lying outdoors in full sunlight makes it difficult to visualise the vocal cords using the relatively weak, battery-powered light attached to our laryngoscopes. To overcome this, we would cover our heads with a blanket to block out the direct sunlight (no doubt presenting an odd spectacle to passers-by).

The MICA Panel Examination

The entirety of the MICA course aimed to prepare us to become competent MICA officers; it also prepared us for the final examination, known simply as "the Panel." It was even more daunting than Phase 1. Again, qualified MICA officers had related their Panel experiences and how anxious and intimidated they had felt approching it. Final qualification as a MICA officer depended on successfully passing this test.

The makeup of the Panel changed from time to time. My MICA student group would face a Panel comprising the AOTC senior lecturer, Dr Frank Archer, the cardiology head of the RMH, an intensivist, the RMH Coronary Care charge nurse, and a senior MICA manager. The examination process was usually for each Panel member to fire questions at the examinee, focussing on their particular field of interest. The MICA manager attending was present to ensure that Panel members asked questions within the context of MICA training. Examination included our interpretation of copies of twelve-lead ECGs and cardiac rhythm strips. The Panel would detail the "patient's" condition linked to these, and we were required to outline our planned treatment, taking both into consideration. We would also be presented with scenarios regarding noncardiac conditions (e.g., acute asthma) and be required to provide a deep understanding of asthma etiology, and how we intended to treat a given patient, based on the details we were given. There was no set time limit to complete the Panel examination, but it tended to average about thirty minutes per each examinee.

Relief and Anticlimax

Panel day finally arrived. At the AOTC, we were advised as a group that each MICA student would be called to attend the Panel alphabetically. We would not be advised of our results until some time after the last student's examination was over. Again, we would be advised alphabetically. With my surname towards the end of the alphabet, I wondered whether this was advantageous, as I hoped that the Panel members might be fatigued by the time my turn came. The Panel was held upstairs, and those of us yet to be called waited at the bottom of the stairs, scanning the faces of each student as they came back down, none of whom looked confident or pleased. Most looked pale and exhausted. Each had been sworn to secrecy regarding the Panel's questions, we discovered later, though questions and scenarios varied with for each student.

Late in the afternoon, I was finally called upstairs; my anxiety had only increased during the long wait. I entered the examination room and immediately felt intimidated by the number of examiners and by their professional standing. My memories of what I was asked and by whom are blurred. I was not made to feel uncomfortable, however, and I had the sense that the collective Panel members wanted me to succeed. It became clear, though, that my responses needed to be based on sound knowledge and that any treatments I proposed had to be founded on solid evidence and accurate ECG interpretation. The RMH Coronary Care charge nurse was seated to my left, and I noticed that she nodded her head slightly as I gave my responses. This was the only indication given that I was hopefully on the right track.

Finally, it was over. I returned downstairs to my colleagues to await our results. At last, we were called back upstairs. As I recall, only one student was given a provisional pass, requiring him to return to his MICA unit to further consolidate his learning and experience by an additional period on the MICA roster. Following this period, he would re-sit the examination. My name was called, and I trudged upstairs with leaden legs. I entered the room and only recall Dr Archer saying, "You've done well."

Doug Quilliam and I, representing PAS, were met by the PAS MICA SSO, who congratulated us; suddenly, it was over. After all the study, anxiety, and stress, the end felt anticlimactic. We returned to PAS to be assigned with a MICA TO for the first eight-week consolidation block.

My first MICA TO was Bill Hogg, an experienced, senior MICA officer with a great sense of humour. Bill helped me hone my airway skill, including intubation, and learn how to use a stethoscope correctly to assess a patient's respiratory status. His experience aided me in enhancing my IV insertion techniques and understanding how to choose the right size and type of needle to meet the circumstances. I was pleased to note that my former AO colleagues had accepted me back in my changed role, including those who were hoping for MICA training selection and the few who had previously attempted Phase 1 and, for whatever reason, opted out or failed to progress.

The types of cases I attended with Bill included elderly patients suffering from acute pulmonary oedema (APO), a condition where, due to chronic cardiac disease, the patient's heart no longer pumped effectively, resulting in a dangerous buildup of fluid in the lungs. APO sufferers vary in clinical presentation, from acute shortness of breath (SOB), usually with a degree of audible chest sounds, known as crackles, caused as air passes through fluid, to unconsciousness, with bloody sputum coming from their mouths.

APO treatment included oxygen therapy and IV drugs aimed at promoting diuresis. APO patients in an altered conscious state required positive pressure ventilations via the Kommy inflatable mask. Patients who have deteriorated further may present as virtually nonbreathing and catatonic and require rapid intubation. Patients still alert enough to be fighting to breathe often pushed away our mask, in fear of it further restricting their efforts. The suffering of APO patients was distressing for us to witness; however, we were frequently rewarded when a patient rapidly improved, both in respiratory staus and consciousness. Hospital staff would sometimes look at us with some scepticism when we explained our patient, now fully conscious and only marginally SOB, had only a short time earlier been critically ill.

Being despatched to patients suffering acute asthma episodes was also common, although unlike APO, asthma afflicted the very young through to the very elderly. Paediatric and teenaged patients suffering acute asthma episodes frequently deteriorated rapidly, requiring rapid medical intervention. It was relatively common for MICA in those days to intubate catatonic or unconscious asthma patients. I found managing these young, critically ill patients distressing, although, as in some APO patients, we were often rewarded with rapid improvement prior to reaching hospital or if, when we returned to the hospital, we found our patient conscious and sitting up in bed.

Introduction to MICA came with becoming accustomed to the 10/14 roster. The two ten-hour day shifts were not difficult to manage, but the two fourteen-hour night shifts were long and seemed never-ending. To compensate for the length of night shifts, as described earlier, the MICA night-shift crew were expected to travel from Frankston to Chelsea at about 11 p.m., to hopefully spend the night. Having spent so many AO nightshifts (albeit of shorter duration) trying to nod off in a chair, it seemed unnatural to be provided actual beds for our exclusive use.

Night shifts at Chelsea were shared with the Chelsea AO night-shift crew, guys we knew well, including their habits. One Chelsea member had over the years become very set in his ways. Towards the end of each and every night shift, he prepared a breakfast for one (invariably, two fried eggs and bacon rashers). Of course, his meal could be disturbed by the controller requiring the crew for a late case. When this occurred, he always erupted with a string of expletives. My next MICA TO was Alan Perrins, who at the time had the distinction of being the youngest Victorian AO to become MICA qualified. Like Bill, Alan possessed a wicked sense of humour. At Chelsea early one morning, we noticed that the AO crew (which included the aforementioned colleague) were out on a case. We decided to have some juvenile fun by taking his eggs out of the fridge, boiling them, and returning them to the fridge. We were still present when he returned and tried to crack his eggs into a frying pan. He was definitely not amused. We knew it was a lame trick, but we looked for humour wherever we could find it (or make it).

Training and working with Alan was enjoyable; he was enthusiastic and knowledgeable, and being of a similar age, we quickly formed a friendship, which continues today. The cases we attended were largely similar to those I'd shared with Bill, although we sometimes seemed to attract unusual cases. We happened to be driving locally in Frankston on a day shift when we witnessed a man collapse on the footpath. We pulled up, got out, and found he was unconscious. We treated him with oxygen and also attached the three leads of our cardiac monitor-defibrillator to his chest. In the bright sunlight, it was difficult to view the small oscilloscope. I was surprised to find that his cardiac rhythm appeared to be uncommon, one I had only seen in textbooks, known as *Torsades de Pointes* (a variation of Ventricular Tachycardia. It is a life-threatening arrythmia requiring urgent intervention. Alan confirmed that my assessment of the rhythm was correct and asked how I intended to treat the patient. Having no prior experience of patients in this rhythm, I was a little hesitant, knowing also that we were only a few minutes from Frankston Hospital. I suggested we take the conservative route and not defibrillate (shock) him. Alan countered my approach and said that we should, which we did, and I was pleased to see that the patient's rhythm reverted to a normal sinus rhythm; eventually, he made a full recovery. In my later MICA years, I came across this rhythm on a few occasions, and with the confidence gained from this experience, I had no hesitation in defibrillating the patient.

Over the sixteen weeks I trained with both Bill and Alan, we attended many cardiac arrest cases. It was during this time that I learned when it was appropriate to begin, continue, or cease a resuscitation. Bill and Alan always asked my opinion, and I was pleased that my views matched theirs. There were, of course, cases where it was obvious that to attempt a resuscitation was pointless (e.g., patients in rigor mortis or patients at the end stage of terminal disease). Should a patient's medical history or length of downtime be uncertain, we would always carry out a resuscitation. It was our view that we made decisions as the patient's advocate, and in the case of elderly patients, we thought about our own parents and what we would want and expect from them in these circumstances.

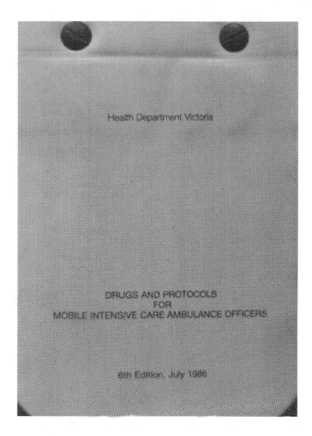

The opening page of the 1986 *MICA Drugs and Protocols* pocket book. The brass screws allowed us to update pages whenever important changes were made.

The Era of Sudden Infant Death Syndrome

In the early 1980s, cases of unexpected baby and infant death, later termed sudden infant death syndrome (SIDS), were growing with alarming frequency. Within PAS' boundaries, SIDS cases seemed to be concentrated in the Dandenong and Cranbourne areas. There was at least one theory which held that this localisation was due to socio-economic reasons. I didn't subscribe to this, as at the majority of cases I attended in these areas, the deceased child had clearly been well cared for. To my knowledge, the concentration of SIDS cases in these areas has never been satisfactorily explained.

In my own experience working on the PAS MICA unit, it seemed at times that each day shift held at least one early-morning suspected SIDS case. The timing coincided with parents waking and checking on their infant. A few especially bad days found us responding to more than one suspected case. Cases ranged from babies just a few days old to children up to the age of three. All cases were tragic, and I don't recall a single successful resuscitation, due largely to the fact that most patients had been found nonbreathing some hours after having been put down to sleep. This uncertain timeframe, from the moment of respiratory arrest to the time the patient was found, was referred to as downtime (also used in adult arrest cases). In cases where we arrived to find such a patient in cardiorespiratory arrest and downtime was uncertain, we always attempted resuscitation, despite the prognosis of a poor outcome. We did this, not only for the patient, but for the parents and siblings, as we wanted to ensure that in future they could look back knowing that every life-saving effort had been made. We would often continue our resuscitation efforts through to arrival at hospital, always where possible taking along one of the parents. In cases where on our arrival, the patient was clearly deceased, advising parents and sometimes siblings was one of the most awful tasks we faced.

Due to parents' efforts to ensure their child remained warm during the night, we usually arrived to find the patient warm, adding to the difficulty of establishing an accurate downtime. The only patients we did not attempt resuscitation were those whose bodies were rigid with rigor mortis.

As in adult cardiorespiratory arrest cases, we treated paediatric cases similarly, through critical interventions such as intubation and adrenaline administration. In adults, adrenaline was usually given intravenously into adult-sized veins. Locating a viable vein in a collapsed paediatric patient was usually impossible. This left us with our only option at the time of administering adrenaline via repeated injections directly into the patient's heart muscle.

To do this required ceasing CPR every few minutes to allow for each required incremental adrenaline dose. Adrenaline was drawn up from a glass ampoule and calculated against the patient's age and weight. The correct anatomical injection site (adjacent to and just to the left of the patient's sternum) was located and marked with a pen. The chest wall was then pierced with a fine-gauge needle, and the attached syringe drawn back until blood was visualised, indicating that the needle had entered a heart chamber. Little imagination is needed to understand how disturbing this action was for the MICA officer, bearing in mind that the needle had to be withdrawn to allow CPR to continue, between each intracardiac injection. The emotions accompanying this action were blackened by the knowledge that our efforts were in all likelihood futile.

On MICA, we frequently carried ambulance observers, including trainee doctors, nurses, and journalists; at PAS, Royal Australian Navy trainee medics based at the Cerberus Naval facility at Hastings (south of Frankston) often attended. One cold morning, we were expecting the arrival of a nurse to accompany us on our day-shift cases. A rather robust young woman duly arrived, dressed in a long overcoat. We barely had time to greet her before we received a despatch to yet another potential SIDS case. As I helped our observer into the rear of the MICA unit, it was evident that she was in the late stages of pregnancy. The SIDS case location was only minutes from our branch; bearing in mind our observer's pregnancy and the likely outcome of the patient, I thought it best that she not enter the scene with us. She was not pleased, but there was no time for a discussion. Coming to the front door, we were met by staff from the Department of Human Services (DHS), who had arrived for a routine welfare check on the single mother and child. The unwitting mother had led them to her child's cot, only to find she was not breathing. Our resuscitation efforts failed, as again the patient's downtime was clearly extensive.

On another occasion, I had arrived early for my shift at Frankston headquarters, noting that all crews were out on cases. To record our shift times, we used an old electronic time clock, into which we inserted our time cards, which would emerge with a time stamp. Below this was fitted a small writing bench. As I began filling out my card, a woman carrying a small bundle came running towards me through the open garage doors. She deposited the bundle on the writing bench; it was immediately evident that it was a baby, nonbreathing, with a blue pallor. As all crews were out, I had virtually no access to any portable resuscitation equipment. I began single-operator CPR and called out to administration staff for assistance. Controllers located a nearby on-shift crew, but again we were defeated by downtime.

Finally, during the 1990s, research pointed to babies having been left to sleep face-down, or on their side, to being a potential likely contributor to causing SIDS. Following this finding, parents were advised to position babies on their back when placing them to rest in their cot. It was thought that there was a risk of a child rebreathing air contaminated by carbon dioxide, within a small area of closed bedding. Parents seemed to quickly embrace and adopt this practice, resulting in a dramatic downturn in case frequency.

Intraosseous Infusions

As described above, cases of paediatric cardiorespiratory arrest were alarmingly common during the 1980s and early 1990s. Resuscitation attempts were always stressful, made more challenging when managing the relative sizes of paediatric airways. Many MICA and non-MICA AOs were at the time parents of young children, adding to the emotions of attending SIDS cases. Nevertheless, we had to put these feelings aside in order to concentrate our efforts on resuscitation and providing support to parents and siblings.

Injecting drugs directly into a child's chest was an extremely intimidating, intimate, and invasive practice. I always felt uncomfortable and queasy when giving intracardiac injections. I was not alone in this, and it was the topic of many discussions I had with my fellow MICA colleague, Paul Livingston. We wondered if there was not an alternative way of effectively administering adrenaline in paediatric cardiorespiratory arrest cases. We had both heard of intraosseous (IO) infusions, a technique whereby a patient's bone marrow is directly accessed via a specialised needle. According to research, the time taken for the body to uptake drug and fluid administration via the IO route was very similar to the IV route. We further researched the history of the IO technique, finding that it had been practised in hospital settings since the 1920s, but not, to our knowledge, in the prehospital setting. The greatest benefit that we could envisage was the end of the era of intracardiac injections.

Over a period of months, Paul and I put together a proposal for the introduction of the IO technique as a new MICA protocol. We presented our submission to the ambulance service's Medical Advisory Board (MAB) in 1991. Our proposal received the MAB's support, which led to the establishment of a mixed medical/ambulance feasibility working group, consisting of the RCH Intensive Care Director, Dr Jim Tibballs, and the Monash Medical Centre Emergency Department Director, Dr Graeme Thomson, and me, representing MICA and MAS. At this time, Paul transferred to a Victorian rural ambulance service, but retained an interest in the group's progress.

The working group met regularly and considered questions such as patient age limitations, training, equipment, and infection control. This work led to a 1992 paper setting out the working group's recommendations to the MAB (see following page).

Erik Schanssema

D RAFT

INTRODUCTION OF INTRAOSSEOUS INFUSION NEEDLES TO MOBILE INTENSIVE CARE AMBULANCE SERVICE

RECOMMENDATIONS

1.   The technique be restricted to the administration of parenteral drugs and vascular volume replacement in true emergencies in infants and children. It may be used after failed attempts at intravenous cannulation but should render intracardiac puncture obsolete. It should be removed as soon as IV access is gained.

2.   The site of needle placement should be the antero-medial surface of the lower tibia although the antero-medial surface of the upper tibia is acceptable.

3.   The technique of insertion should be that described by Spivey WH, J Pediatrics 1987;111:639-643. In summary, the bone marrow is entered by a near-perpendicular approach to the skin surface of the above locations. A rotatory action is necessary to traverse the bone cortex until a distinct sudden loss of resistance is perceived. The usual depth of penetration is 1 cm or less from the skin surface.

4.   The technique should not be used if any part of the limb is traumatised or infected locally or if the anticipated site cannot be cleansed.

5.   Precautions:
     a.   The skin should be sterilised with 70% isopropyl alcohol (current equipment).
     b.   Care should be taken to prevent injection of air.
     c.   Extravasation into skin should be avoided.

6.   The standard equipment needle should be the Cook Australia 16G model with Dieckmann modification. This would limit the purchase costs and still enable use in all ages (no other type of needle is currently available). The handle should be the Australian safety modification - the prototype of which is now being examined by the proponents (refer Dr Bob Wright, ICU, St Vincent's Hospital, Sydney) and which should be available for order in two weeks (refer Mr Gary Trotman, Cook Australia Pty Ltd on 008 777 780). Cost (with Molnar skin stabilisation disk) $30 per item (imported equivalent without safety handle $43). The needle has a proximal Luer lock fitting enabling connection to 3-way taps or IV line.

     The FDA of USA has embargoed the export of needle from USA pending a dispute over the use of "infusion" in the product description. Long term disputation is not anticipated and in any case, the needles are to be manufactured in Brisbane.

7.   Teaching the technique may be accomplished with the aid of pork ribs. Existing models may be used for teaching and practice.

Erik Schanssemma   Jim Tibballs   Graema Thomson
MICA   Paediatric Intensivist   Emergency Physician
                          Royal Children's Hospital Monash Medical Centre
                          Melbourne   Melbourne

4 Feb 1992

A copy of the IO recommendation paper (note the spelling error in Dr Thomson's first name).

128

On behalf of the IO working group, I was invited to present our proposal at the Paediatrics Workshop of the MICA Drugs and Protocols Review panel, at the offices of DHS. The panel accepted and endorsed our proposal, including the draft of the new MICA protocol and the associated training plan. All MICA paramedics were subsequently trained in the correct technique using the Cook's 16 gauge IO needle shown below. Insertion requires the needle (hence the large palm grip) to be inserted through the skin, continuing in a twisting motion, until it "gives," a sensation felt as it enters bone marrow. Practice was conducted using pork ribs, which approximated the depth and resistance encountered, relative to a human paediatric leg.

Two anatomical sites were determined to be the best and safest for successful IO needle placement. Both sites ensured that if successfully inserted, the needle should remain firmly in place and was unlikely to be accidentally dislodged during further treatment and pateint transport. Specifically, these sites were on the small flat plane of the upper tibia, just below the knee, or the lower tibia, just above the ankle. A guide marking the correct depth at which bone penetration should occur is marked towards the end of the needle. Once successfully in place, the palm grip is unscrewed, removed, and replaced with an IV line, through which both drugs and fluids could be administered.

2. INTRAOSSEOUS INFUSION

INDICATIONS

Venous access may be difficult particularly in the collapsed, hypovolaemic or hypothermic child. The priority is to restore spontaneous cardiac output as rapidly as possible and the use of intraosseous infusion of drugs is justified in children, if an intravenous line cannot be inserted without undue delay. This technique is to be restricted to the administration of parenteral drugs and vascular volume replacement in true emergencies in infants and children.

CONTRAINDICATIONS

This technique should not be used if any part of the limb is traumatised or infected, or if the proposed site cannot be adequately cleansed.

TECHNIQUE

The site of needle placement should be the antero-medial surface of the lower tibia, although the antero-medial surface of the upper tibia is acceptable.

The bone marrow is entered by a near perpendicular approach to the skin surface of the above locations, angling away from the epiphysis. A rotary action is necessary to traverse the bone cortex until a distinct sudden loss of resistance is perceived. The usual penetration is less than 1cm from the skin surface.

PRECAUTIONS

1. The skin should be sterilised with 70% isopropyl alcohol
2. Care should be taken not to inject air
3. Beware of extravasation into the skin
4. Wear sterile gloves to prevent causing bony infection

COMPLICATIONS

1. Infection of bony tissue
2. Necrosis of surrounding soft tissue due to extravasation
3. Pain at time of insertion

The MICA Protocol for Intraosseous Infusions from the 1994 MICA handbook.

The MICA Intraosseous Infusion protocol was first used operationally by a MAS MICA crew in July 1992. To monitor the protocol on behalf of MICA, I was asked to review and collate each IO attempt, whether successful or not. The first six attempts were successful; however, it was reported that during resuscitation attempts, as the fluid bag attached to the IV drained via gravity alone, it sometimes stopped running. Blood in the bone marrow does not flow as freely as blood in veins. All MICA paramedics were subsequently advised to wrap a blood pressure cuff around the fluid bag and inflate it to a low pressure. This action largely solved the problem, although in patients with congenital bone disorders, both IO needle insertion and the maintenance of IV drugs or fluid could be problematic. Fortunately, such cases were rare.

From the introduction of the MICA IO protocol in 1992 through to 1996, MICA had employed the technique on thirty-two patients, ranging in age from one week old to a single case of a fourteen-year-old. The following table provides a summary of these cases:

Average patient age: 29.4 months
Number of patients receiving continued treatment to hospital: 20
Patients' presenting problems:
Cardiorespiratory arrest: 23
Cardiorespiratory arrest due to traumatic injuries: 2
Electromechanical dissociation (EMD*): 3
Electromechanical dissociation in trauma: 2
Ventricular fibrillation (VF**): 2

* A condition in which there is cardiac electrical activity but in the absence of cardiac pumping

** Chaotic electrical impulses in the absence of effective cardiac pumping, requiring defibrillation

In September 1996, I was invited to present details of MICA's 1992–1996 IO experience to the 2nd International "Spark of Life" conference held at Melbourne's World Congress Centre. The late Dr Jeff Wassertheil graciously offered to compile the MAS IO data into a Powerpoint presentation for my presentation.

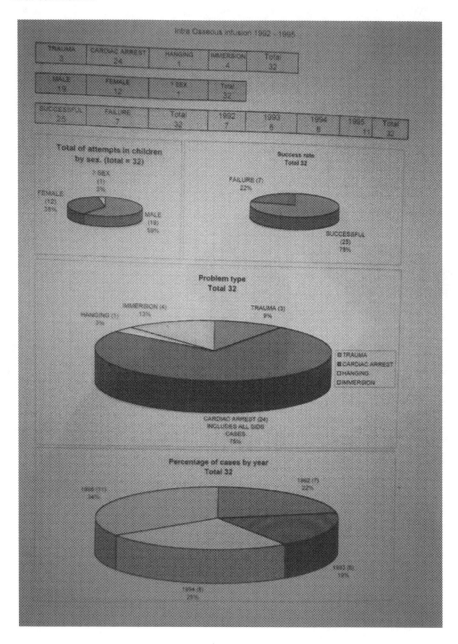

Drag Racing

Some of the most severe vehicle crashes I attended occurred in the greater Dandenong area. Certain roads were well known for late-night inpromptu drag races. The first case described unusually took place during daylight hours. Two vehicles were involved and had apparently been racing at high speed, side by side, when one lost control, flipping over. As it rolled, the driver was momentarily impaled on a wooden picket fence. The vehicle finished up on its wheels on the lawn.

We arrived to find a male unconscious, still in the driver's seat. His chest had been torn open, exposing a clavicle (collar bone), upper ribs, and upper lung lobes, which were bubbling air and blood, emitting a hissing sound. His throat was also badly torn. Securing his airway was our first priority, and as extricating him from the vehicle would take up valuable time, we decided to intubate him in situ. This was successful, but there was little we could do for his extensive chest and neck injuries. We alerted Dandenong Hospital of our patient's condition and injuries, advising the hospital that we expected to arrive there shortly. A trauma team was waiting for us, but if I recall correctly, the patient did not survive long.

Late at night, another drag race occurred on the same stretch of road, involving two vehicles, which again had been travelling at speed. We arrived to find the wrecked vehicles separated by a distance of about a hundred metres. We split up, and as we were the first ambulance on scene, we shared our portable equipment as best we could. My vehicle had been sliced in two as it slid into a wooden power pole. The driver and front-seat passenger were not seriously injured, but the left rear passenger sat fully exposed in the vehicle's rear half. He had taken the full force of the vehicle slamming into the power pole between his legs. He was in an altered conscious state, and his lower abdomen was split open from his genitals through to his lower back. Fortunately, because of his position, he was easy to remove. Again there was not a great deal we could do for him; he obviously required urgent surgery. We advised Dandenong Hospital of his condition, but he died at the hospital.

◼ More Tragedies

Travelling at night with a friend, a young woman's car struck a horse that had escaped from a nearby field. We arrived to find her car buried in a huge mound of mixed gorse intestines and undigested grass— much of which had also flooded the car's interior through the smashed windscreen.

The horse had crushed the roof as it rolled over the top, landing dead on the roadway. We made our way through the slippery mess to assess the occupants. The driver had survived and luckily was unable to see her friend beside her, as the roof had caved in, separating them. The driver had suffered relatively minor injuries, but her friend had been killed, her neck broken over the seat's backrest, her head nearly severed. The combined smell of human blood, horse intestines, and undigested grass was overpowering.

On another shift but with the same colleague, we were despatched to a shooting in the Dandenong area. A middle-aged woman, alone in her daughter's home, had apparently been helping out with housekeeping when two men burst in. At least one was armed with a shotgun. A struggle ensued, and the shotgun discharged, firing through a small pillow they had placed over her chest. Fortunately, it appeared that she had turned away as she was shot, blowing a hole through the pillow and leaving her with a large hole completely through her left breast, but not piercing her chest wall. Her attackers had left, and we covered up her wounds, treated her pain, and transported her to Dandenong Hospital, where I believe she recovered.

Many of us supplemented our incomes by accepting overtime shifts. I received a call from the MAS rosters department one day, not long after I had returned home, having completed my two fourteen-hour night shifts. I agreed to work a third fourteen-hour night shift at a MICA unit in Melbourne's north.

At first, the shift was quiet, until nearing midnight, we were despatched to a car crash. We arrived to find a sedan had run off a suburban street, struck a brick fence, and rolled onto its side. The driver was walking about the scene, appearing dazed and confused, but otherwise uninjured. Looking into the car, I saw two other patients, one on top of the other, both with extensive head injuries. Three further patients occupied the back seat, again stacked on top of each other, all with apparent head and internal injuries. The body of a young male lay between the car's rear and the brick fence. We discovered that he had been travelling in the car's boot, which had burst open on impact, flinging his body into the brick fence.

The scene was very busy, as we worked to further assess and prioritise our patients; fortunately, other MAS crews arrived to assist us. When it was over and I had retrieved our portable equipment, I realised I had left something behind. I walked back the short distance to the scene, stepping over police tapes set up to restrict entry to what was now a crime scene. A police officer challenged me and told me I couldn't enter the scene. I blame my fatigue and the stress of the case, but I responded sarcastically, "You've got to be kidding, I've been in there for the past hour!" Apologies to him, as he was only doing his job. Working with other emergency services was always conducted in a consultative, collaborative manner, each understanding and respecting the roles of the other.

One night, we had just made the routine night-shift journey from PAS Frankston headquarters to Chelsea branch, hoping to get some rest. We managed to lie down for a short period but were despatched to a nearby siege situation. We arrived within a few minutes to find members of the Victoria Police Special Operations Group (SOG) waiting for us, heavily armed. I was jockey for the night and was advised that a man was holding a woman hostage in a room at the rear of the address.

The senior SOG officer asked my name and advised me to wait with my portable equipment at the end of the driveway. Within moments, there was a loud crash, followed by my name being called. I made my way down the long driveway and into a completely dark room, lit only by SOG torches. The crash I had heard was the result of the door being smashed open with a sledgehammer. The alleged hostage-taker was lying face-up, just inside the doorway. His eyes were shut, but his eyelids were flickering; I was certain he was feigning unconsciousness. I noticed a small pool of blood in the hollow of his throat and a bloodied screwdriver beside him. The hostage was uninjured and had been taken from the room. As I examined my patient, a blacked-out SOG officer stood over him, the barrel of his automatic weapon quivering just centimetres above the patient's chest. I was kneeling directly over the patient, hoping that he wouldn't make any sudden movements; the SOG officer seemed tense and on edge. It appeared that the patient had pierced his throat with the screwdriver as police broke down the door, although his injury was not life-threatening. We transported him to Frankston Hospital, with police escort.

On another night at Chelsea branch, we received a call in the early hours of the morning to respond to a shooting, only a few streets away. Our controller could not advise us if police were present. Under the circumstances and despite being despatched Signal 8, we decided to travel without lights and sirens. A street or two from the case location, we briefly noticed a man passing beneath a street light, wearing what appeared to be a white pullover, the front of which had large, dark stains. We suspected he may have been the gunman, although we didn't spot a weapon, and we assumed that the stains were, in fact, blood.

A minute or so later, we arrived at the address given, finding a caravan parked at the front of the address, with its lights on. I got out and looked inside, seeing a woman slumped in a corner, covered in blood and clearly deceased. A rifle lay nearby on a bench. The sight of her, which I can easily conjure up today,was shocking. I could only imagine the fear and terror she must have experienced prior to being shot.

Returning home from night-shift cases such as these and trying to sleep was always difficult. Sometimes, when I didn't have to come in for a subsequent night shift, I would stay awake for the day, hoping to sleep through the coming night.

HIV and AIDS

In the early 1980s, the spectre of HIV and AIDS swept around the world, accompanied by great anxiety, fear, and confusion regarding its origins. This was also felt by people working in the medical field. Wider society, searching for a scapegoat, pointed prejudiced fingers at the gay community and at those who injected illicit drugs.

For paramedics, it meant that from the time we were first alerted to risks associated with potential HIV infection, each patient would need to be approached as being HIV positive. It took some time and further understanding to realise that the threat to us was minimal; nevertheless, we need to take infection control practices seriously, particularly when in contact with blood and body fluid. With few exceptions, we wore disposable gloves and protective glasses any time there was an exposure risk. In trauma cases such as car crashes, where we are faced with torn metal and other sharp edges, many of us wore double layers of disposable gloves.

Most concerning for us was the very real risk of inadvertently sustaining a needle stick injury and acquiring HIV or hepatitis through cross contamination. Although instances were few, needle stick injuries did occur, usually in the setting of a time-critical case where there was frequent and rapid movement of paramedics and equipment. If paramedics were unfortunate enough to sustain such an injury, they were subjected to six months of ongoing blood tests, at the end of which, hopefully, they would be declared infection free. During this long period, the injured paramedic, partner, and family would be left anxious and in doubt. I am not aware of any MAS paramedic who suffered a needle stick injury actually acquiring an infection. For paramedics, though, in constant contact with patients, the fear was very real and remained in the forefronts of our minds.

I was always extremely disciplined and focussed when using needles. One day, though, we received a despatch to a seven-year-old boy who was in suspected cardiac arrest. The child was suffering from a chronic congenital blood disorder and had been at home when he suddenly collapsed, bleeding orally. Calls to paediatric arrests always provoked anxiety, but whilst en route, we tried to concentrate on recalling the appropriate drug doses and ETT sizes that we might need.

As I've previously described, locating a viable vein in a collapsed paediatric patient was difficult if not impossible. In adult patients in cardiac arrest, our first option was to find a large vein in the so-called cubital fossa (the skin surface between the forearm and the upper arm). Where this fails, we would attempt to insert an IV cannula into a carotid vein in the patient's neck; these usually remain prominent despite cardiac arrest. To do this in a child is more difficult, given the size of the patient's head relative to his or her body. Such was the case with the patient I was presented with. In an effort to overcome this, I bent an appropriate sized needle to about 30 degrees, meaning that when I inserted it, it would enter parallel to the patient's neck. I successfully inserted it, only for it to be accidentally dislodged, piercing my thumb through the thin disposable glove.

I was immediartely flooded with thoughts about the potential implications but had to remain focussed on our resuscitation efforts. Employing the same technique, I inserted a replacement needle, and the resuscitation continued. Sadly, we were not rewarded with a returned heartbeat, and bearing in mind the patient's downtime, we eventually decided to stop and advised the parents that nothing further could be done.

I subsequently endured the six months of blood tests and waiting, at the end of which I was finally cleared of infection. The experience, though, only served to increase my overall anxiety when dealing with needles and patients with blood or body fluid loss.

As I describe in the Author's Note, in 1986, I suffered a sudden decompensation crisis, which I was informed was the new way of describing a nervous breakdown. Decompensation crisis, though, better describes what takes place when the psyche has reached a point where it cannot absorb any further stress, and both body and mind collapse. My psychiatrist also diagnosed me with obsessive compulsive disorder (OCD), a term at the time completely foreign to me and something that took me years to accept.

Whether or not my illness was at the root cause, I found myself becoming increasingly anxious when dealing with patients who were potentially HIV positive. I became obsessed with ensuring whatever ambulance vehicle I was using at the time was clean and free of blood stains. To protect my family, and aware of what I might have stepped in during a shift, I always took the precaution of removing my work footwear and depositing it by the front door when I returned home.

Any case that a paramedic attends, whether minor or significant, may result in unanticipated physical injury or psychological impact. For me, it occurred many years into my MICA career, during a time when I had the dual responsibilities of managing my MICA team and concurrently training a MICA student. We were despatched to a shooting case at a private suburban address. We arrived, noting police were not yet in attendance. We were met by the patient's brother, who was clearly in distress. He showed us into the living room, where we were confronted by a young, unconscious adult male, lying face-up on the floor. He had a large hole to the left centre of his chest, and beside him lay a single-barrel shotgun. We noticed a hole in the ceiling, where he had apparently test-fired the weapon. As he shot himself, he fell back onto a glass coffee table, causing it to shatter.

I was struck by the quantity of blood on and around the patient and the pieces of what appeared to be lung tissue. Despite the severity of his wound, he was breathing, albeit erratically. There was no way to begin further assessment and treatment without kneeling in his blood and tissue. For the first time in my career, I was suddenly and acutely aware that I did not want to do this particular job. My student was looking to me for direction, and so I asked him to begin by managing the patient's airway. I felt powerless and angry with myself, as I did not want to get involved in the hands-on treatment of the patient. I had a reputation, or so I believed, for never hesitating in assessing and treating a patient regardless of circumstances.

We both knew that the patient's injuries were nonsurvivable, expecting him to expire at any moment. I forced myself to participate, but soon the patient arrested, and to attempt resuscitation would have been pointless. I admit to feeling somehow relieved; at the same time, I felt ashamed of my initial reluctance.

Some cases, despite our training and equipment, left us feeling completely helpless. Such was the case when we were despatched to a suspected overdose in an affluent suburb. The case details we were provided were scant. We arrived at a private residence, where we were met by the patient's distraught partner. He showed us into the kitchen, where we saw a young woman about thirty years of age, sitting on top of a kitchen bench, where her partner had placed her after finding her on the floor. My initial sight of her is imprinted on my memory. She was conscious, looking directly at me, unable to speak, with copious black vomitus coming from her mouth and down her front, and on the kitchen floor. Her partner told us that she had consumed a bottle of drain cleaning solution, followed by a bottle of bleach. She had regurgitated the contents and in the process severely burnt her mouth and tongue, leaving her unable to speak. She did not appear to be in pain but wore a bewildered, resigned expression. Her vital signs were in acceptable limits, and the best and only real option for us was to transport her to hospital as quickly as we could.

We placed her on our stretcher and left for a major city hospital, which was only minutes away. She appeared most comfortable sitting upright on the stretcher. Her eyes never left me during the trip, and I held her hand, trying to give her some words of encouragement, although we both knew her death was near. We had advised the hospital of her condition, and staff were waiting for us as we arrived. I had to leave her there, as she was immediately taken to an operating theatre, where I was informed later that her entire alimentary system had been destroyed. She died soon after, still in theatre.

The following day, I was approached at the same hospital by one of the senior nurses. I had known her for many years, and we got along fine, despite her reputation for being cold and critical of junior nurses and sometimes for venting her wrath on paramedics. She was aware of the previous day's case, but I was surprised and touched when she asked me if I was okay. I wasn't, and for months and years after the case, I wondered if there was more I could have done for my patient.

At the time, the role of a MICA team manager (TM) included working on the 10/14 roster and often also training a MICA student. It was only sometime later that we were granted a single day, known as a function day, to accomplish our administrative duties, including clinically reviewing each case attended by my team.

Needless Death

At around midnight on a winter night, we were despatched to provide back-up to assist the single on-call paramedic of a peripheral branch. He had been despatched to a crash, believed to be serious. Our journey, using lights and sirens, took over thirty minutes. We arrived to find a utility and a station wagon had struck head-on at high speed on an unsealed road. We both knew the on-call paramedic well. He was experienced and reliable and consistently accurate in his patient assessments.

Beneath and under the front wheels of the utility was the body of a young male. I looked into the station wagon, which at first appeared unoccupied, although I spotted a bundle under the passenger side of the dashboard. Under torchlight, I saw that it was, in fact, a person wearing a bulky padded jacket. I examined the patient, a female perhaps twenty years of age, but she had clearly died on impact.

My MICA colleague then sought my assistance with another patient who was unconscious, suffering significant head and chest injuries. The police/ambulance helicopter (designated AIR 495, see photo) had also been despatched and would further treat and transport this patient. Yet another patient had been located in the dark, although his injuries were not life-threatening. We transported him to Dandenong Hospital. If I recall correctly, it was he who informed us that the deceased woman was pregnant and due to be induced the following day, at Dandenong Hospital. Her pregancy was not obvious, as the force of the impact had caused her to be compressed into a bundled shape where I found her.

At Dandenong Hospital, I retired to the staff room to write up my patient's patient care record (PCR). A nurse who I knew well came in for her break and asked me about the case. I explained the tragic circumstances of the deceased female, including her planned inducement for the following day. She surprised me by asking why I hadn't cut the baby from the mother's abdomen and attempted a resuscitation. I was completely taken aback by her question, especially as it came from a very experienced nurse. I explained further that the patient was killed outright by the impact, which had occurred more than thirty minutes prior to our arrival; therefore, the impact would also have killed her unborn child. I felt it unnecessary, but I advised her that there was no way we would consider an impromptu caesarian. We certainly didn't possess the training or the equipment for such an emergency operation.

I had believed that we had done a good job under difficult cicumstances; however, her question introduced an element of doubt. I knew categorically, though, that there was no hope for the foetus, given both the severity and speed of the crash and the fact that the mother-to-be had been killed outright.

This Is Going to Hurt!

During my operational career, ambulance crashes seldom occurred, although one incident served as a stark reminder never to take our safety on the road for granted. I was the jockey on a day shift at the MICA 7 unit at Dandenong, when we were despatched to meet one of our peripheral colleagues, who was managing a time-critical patient on his own.

It was early January, and overnight, Melbourne had received its first summer rain for the new year. Our station officer (SO) had decided to come along to observe, as he sometimes did, and buckled himself into the rear seat. This position provided very limited forward view.

My colleague was a sensible, safe driver, and we made our way up into the Dandenong ranges, travelling under Signal 8 conditions. It was early morning, and the roads were still damp. As we headed down the slight incline of a sealed road, we came to a gradual left-hand bend, requiring the use of brakes. As these were applied, instead of following the bend, we continued straight on, over the edge of the road and down a steep embankment through a large open property. There was silence among us as my colleague tried to maintain a straight heading on the soft, wet earth.

We continued down, picking up speed until we saw a house at the bottom of the slope and to the immediate left of which was a large chicken pen; it seemed we were going to hit one or the other. I remember thinking quite calmly that I expected we'd be injured. We struck the side of the house, a glancing blow, but sufficient to stop us. Our ambulance, having destroyed some plumbing, came to rest against the house. We looked around at each other, relieved to end up uninjured.

The experience was even worse for our intrepid SO, as he couldn't see much of what was happening as we headed down hill. The lady of the house emerged and very pleasantly asked if we'd like a cup of tea! She explained that she and her husband had been lying in bed, watching us come down the hill. She said we'd been extremely lucky, as it was only during the previous week that they had had a large gum tree removed, which otherwise would have been directly in our path.

I didn't have any further time to contemplate our luck, as our peripheral colleague arrived at the top of hill. I collected some of our portable equipment and headed back up the hill to assist him. I have no recollection of his patient's condition, let alone what treatment I gave; nevertheless, we made it safely to Dandenong Hospital, where the news of our crash was already spreading. No matter how many times, then and later, that we denied demolishing the chicken pen, this is what everyone believed. I guess it made for a better story.

Sometimes, as if it were somehow predetermined, some paramedics seemed to attract certain types of cases. In my case, I seemed to be frequently attending to very ill or deceased children. I also seemed to attract suicide cases, which were commonly hangings. During the early 1990s, there was a period of about eight months where I attended six suicides by hanging. Each, of course, was tragic, but they were never the same. In one case, an elderly man who had just lost his wife to cancer and who was himself frail nevertheless found a means to end his life. He had rolled a portable barbeque from his backyard into his home. He then tied a belt to its lifting rail and then around his neck. He knelt down and simply leaned forward until he was asphyxiated. There was no indication at all that he had struggled.

On another occasion during this period, we were called to a suicide in an apartment building. A middle-aged man had been watching TV in his living room when he heard a sudden crashing noise coming from the main bedroom. There he found his wife hanging from a rail, inside a wardrobe. We attempted her resuscitation but were ultimately unsuccessful.

Also during this period, we were called to another suspected suicide, the date coinciding with the public release of the inquest into the death of INXS singer, Michael Hutchence. We arrived to find the deceased body of a young man who had hung himself with a belt attached to his doorknob. According to his partner, who had been studying in an adjoining room, he had copied the method he believed the late Mr Hutchence had used; large posters of the singer covered his bedroom walls.

Amongst this sequence of suicides was another that, no less tragic, left me feeling bewildered and angry. A male, perhaps in his early thirties, had removed a ceiling trap door leading to an under-roof storage area; he tied a rope to one of the roof supporting beams and hung himself. He was found by his two children when they arrived home from primary school. We can never know what motivated their father, but it seemed to us that he had planned his timing deliberately. I was already distressed by this case and had returned to our ambulance parked at the front of the residence when I noticed bright flashes coming from the home opposite. It was obvious that someone was photographing the scene. Without thinking about it any further, or asking police present to intervene, I walked up to the front door, knocked, and expressed my disgust to the occupant.

Despatched to yet another suspected suicide, we arrived at a suburban home and were directed into the large two-car garage. A middle-aged male hung from a rope attached to a roof beam. He was wearing only a woman's nightie and had set up a stepladder between two cars, both of which had erotic magazines open on their bonnets. We surmised that this was an auto-erotic act that had gone tragically wrong. His body had been found by his son, who appeared to be about twelve years of age. I hated attending hanging cases, regardless of circumstances.

▌ Team Manager

I was appointed as a MICA Team Manager in 1990, not long after the amalgamation of PAS and ASM into MAS. Team manager was the term used to replace the very long-standing title of station officer. At the same time, the term "branch" was changed to "team." For the next decade, I was to serve as TM at MICA 2, located in the grounds of the Alfred Hospital, MICA 7, adjacent to the MAS Dandenong Team location and across the car park of Dandenong Hospital, at a trial Clayton Paramedic Response Unit (PRU), crews consisting of a MICA paramedic and non-MICA paramedic, colocated with the MAS Springvale Team, itself colocated with the Springvale Country Fire Authority (CFA) branch and finally at MICA 11, a newly established team (replacing the Clayton PRU), located in a Clayton industrial estate.

My favourite location, though, was MICA 7 (see photo), where MICA lived and worked out of the former Dandenong SO's residence. I always felt more at home here, as I knew the area and the paramedics at Dandenong and surrounding branches and the Dandenong and surrounding hospitals' staff. One of the most competent (in the collective opinion of local paramedics) doctors at the accident and emergency (formerly casualty) department of Dandenong Hospital possessed a thick Eastern European accent. He had a wonderful sense of humour, and if we arrived with a patient he deemed should not have been transported to hospital and was better seen by a GP, his standard question was, "Vot did you bring that in here for?" Of course, he realised that we often had no option other than to apply a risk averse approach when assessing a patient outside of the hospital environment. Better to be safe than sorry from both the patient's and our perspective. He was never disappointed should we arrive with a trauma case, which was his particular bent.

A photo of the first MICA 7 team, prior to my becoming the TM. Left to right are Rob Fergusson, Paul Livingston, Ron MacIntosh, Peter Ballard, SO Ian Donaldson, Russell Nelson, Rob Ray, Jeff Allen, Brian

Fallows, myself, Don White, and visiting MICA SO Laurie Spelling. Part of Dandenong team's location is in the background.

The Great MICA 7 versus Dandenong Team Battle

Now and then, both the MICA 7 and Dandenong team crews would let off steam by playing pranks on each other. I happened to be standing in MICA 7's kitchen in the middle of a hot summer day when I looked up to see two of our Dandenong colleagues running across the driveway separating our adjoining buildings, both wearing pillow cases, with cut-outs for their eyes. Between them, they were carrying their high-powered fire hose. I had only time to shut our back door, before they opened the large brass nozzle and turned it, full force, onto the door. The water struck with enough force that it found its way under and between any gaps, quickly flooding the laundry and kitchen floors. They ran off before we could retaliate, but we were not fooled by their pathetic disguises; one of them was easily recognisable by his hirsute forearms.

They knew retribution would follow, but we bided our time, hoping to increase their anxiety. Both were on shift the following night, and we waited for them to be despatched, providing us with an opportunity to restore MICA 7's honour. We decided to focus our attention on the ringleader, who was a keen cyclist. Finally, they were despatched, and we opened their garage doors and found his bike, which we hoisted via ropes up and out of reach into the roof girders. Not done, we had brought along a 50ml syringe of 50 percent Dextrose, a clear viscous sugar solution used in the treatment of patients in diabetic coma. We emptied the contents into his personal shampoo bottle and slunk away. Nothing further was heard from the crew, and with our dignity restored, peace broke out.

Choices

On a hot Janauary evening, we were despatched to a possible immersion (drowning) case in a small lake within the bounds of a public golf course. We arrived at the clubhouse to be directed by staff to the lake and found two or three teenagers, standing by the water's edge in damp clothing. They were pointing towards the centre of the lake. They and an additional friend had apparently decided to cool offf in the lake, but one of them had failed to resurface. No one was in the water or preparing to attempt locating him. My partner and I quickly discussed what we would do, and I said I would go in.

I stripped off my uniform and shoes and entered the very murky water, finding that it was quite warm on the surface, but icy cold below a few centimetres. I swam out into the middle, to where the boys had been pointing. The depth of the water was over my head, so I tried diving down a number of times but could neither see nor feel anything. I realised too that I was tiring quickly in the cold water.

Two golfers came to my aid, swimming out to meet me. I suggested we try a line search. After a short time, one of them said that he thought he could feel something with his toes. I asked him not to move. Between the three of us, we managed to get a grip on the patient's clothing and pulled him up to the surface. By now, I was exhausted and so asked them if they could pull the body back to the lake edge, where my colleague was waiting. I was now concerned for myself, still out in the middle, cold and spent, wondering if I'd made the right decision to go in.

I slowly got back, and we assessed our patient, who was about seventeen years of age. Calculating our despatch time and checking with the patient's friends, we estimated that he'd been under water for over an hour. We decided not to attempt a resuscitation. AIR 495 appeared overhead, and we waved them off. An SSO arrived on scene, and I advised him what we had done. His response was basically that we should return to MICA 7 for a shower before continuing with our shift.

Following this case and despite the danger I put myself in, I have always believed I had made the right decision, both for me and the patient. I could not just have stood by and done nothing, despite knowing the likely outcome if we could find him. Having said this, it was a personal decision, and I would not expect others to follow my lead if faced with a similar scenario.

Multiple Shooting

As previously noted, both MICA and AO crews commonly carried observers as part of their medical, hospital, or naval training. MICA 7 had a close working and personal relationship with the medical and nursing staff of the Dandenong Hospital Coronary Care Unit (CCU). One of the senior CCU nurses often joined us for an observer shift, more for her own interest than as part of any required training. Observers who spent an afternoon and evening with us were expected to leave before midnight, allowing us the opportunity for rest, if we were fortunate enough. She happened to be with us late one evening when we were despatched to a suspected shooting in a nearby suburb. As we were away from our MICA 7 residence, she would have to come along.

Arriving close to the scene, we noticed many police in attendance. Nearby, we were shown to a conscious adult male, sitting on the curb. He had suffered multiple gunshot wounds to his face, evidently fired at very close range. Incredibly, none seemed to have penetrated his skull. I was uncomfortable arriving at a shooting scene, having the additional responsibility for our observer's safety and welfare. I recall asking a police officer if the location of the gunman was known; she replied that they were certain he'd left the scene. Nevertheless, I had asked our observer to wait in our vehicle. We treated our patient and transported him to hospital but were immediately despatched to another case, still carrying our observer. An hour or so later, we were at Monash Medical Centre when, to our surprise, we were recalled to the shooting scene, as another victim had been located.

Arriving back on scene, the area around the shooting had been sealed off, and TV crews were present, held back at a safe distance. Again, I asked our observer to wait in our vehicle. Police directed us down the same street that we had first attended, pointing to a figure lying on the nature strip. A woman, about thirty years of age, lay on her back, dead from gunshot wounds.

Police in the home directly behind her showed us to a large male, probably in his thirties. He was standing up but had suffered a large gunshot wound to his forehead, apparently self-inflicted. He was agitated and walked unprompted out of the front door; without direction, he lay on our stretcher, which we'd left on the driveway. As he was the alleged gunman, it seemed clear that he had remained at the scene at the time we treated his first victim. We treated and transported him to Dandenong Hospital, from where he was later transferred to a major city hospital, where he underwent a frontal lobotomy, necessary due to his penetrating head injury. Finally, our observer was able to leave us and pick up her car, which had been left at MICA 7.

▋ Unwanted Professional "Assistance"

Late one summer afternoon, we were despatched to a two-vehicle collision outside a suburban shopping centre. A large crowd had gathered, and as we approached, I happened to spot the unusual sight of a man standing on a car's bonnet, observing the scene. We saw that two cars had crashed at an intersection controlled by traffic lights. A non-MICA crew had arrived prior to us and were busy assessing the patients. One of the crew asked me to check out one of the cars. I found the driver, a young adult male, dead, his head crushed by the caved-in roof. His neck appeared to be fractured, as his head was positioned awkwardly over the seat's back.

A bystander appeared next to me, introducing himself as an anaesthetist. I believe that he was the person I'd seen standing on the car's bonnet. He told me that he wanted to access our equipment so that he could intubate the patient. I told him that the patient was dead, but he insisted. I reiterated that the patient was definitely deceased and that he was interrupting our efforts to assist other patients. At this time, one of my colleagues called out that he needed help. Ignoring the anaesthetist, I moved across to the other car, where my colleagues were busy with a male patient in his twenties, conscious but acutely short of breath. Excluding a possible tension pneumothorax, I was concerned that the force of the impact to his chest and abdomen had ruptured his diaphragm, resulting in a traumatic diaphragmatic hernia. In such cases, a patient's abdominal contents are forced through the diaphragmatic tear, resulting in shortness of breath and potentially compromising blood flow to internal organs. His injuries were time-critical and required urgent surgical intervention. Whilst treating this patient, I caught sight of the anaesthetist attempting intubation on the deceased patient, using our equipment. An MAS SSO arrived on scene, and I briefly described my interaction with the anaesthetist. I asked him to speak him and obtain his details, including the hospital he worked for.

We left for hospital with our patient, who it was later confirmed had suffered a traumatic diaphragmatic hernia, although I'm unaware of his eventual outcome.

Several weeks later, I heard from the ambulance service medical officer, himself an anaesthetist, who had managed to contact and speak with the anaesthetist, no doubt expressing his concerns regarding his actions.

19

The Millennium Bug

As the world edged towards the beginning of the twenty-first century, many will recall the near-hysteria regarding the so-called Millennium Bug. Otherwise rational scientists and computer specialists speculated that the Internet, other electronically based information systems, and public utilities would crash as digital clocks within computers ticked over; the digital figure 2000 would not be recognised, and computers would revert to the year 1900.

Partly due to this angst and uncertainty, it was expected that larger-than-usual New Year's Eve (NYE) crowds would gather to witness whatever might happen as midnight struck. In Melbourne, traditionally the largest gatherings of NYE revellers are at city locations, particularly along the Yarra River, where fireworks barges unleash at midnight. MAS planned to ensure that sufficient resources were available to deal with the larger-than-expected crowds. To supplement MAS on road crews, a plan was devised whereby three MICA TMs would be deployed on police boats at intervals along the Yarra. As cases occurred along the river banks, they would step off their assigned boat and carry their portable equipment directly to the patients. In principle, the concept seemed sound, albeit untried.

The three MICA TMs were to be Ian Hunt, Doug Quilliam, and me. On the evening of NYE, we gathered at St Kilda marine, where the police boats were moored. We departed and motored across the top of Port Phillip Bay and entered the Yarra River mouth. Ian and Doug were deployed along the stretch of river which included the Crown Casino and Jing and Flinders Street bridges. I was to be deployed further east up to the Swan Street bridge at Richmond. As I was preparing my equipment, I was advised that my assigned police boat had broken down—perhaps the Millennium Bug had its first victim. There were no spare police boats available; however, a river service boat was able to fill the breach.

Captain, My Captain

The service boat was of a two-seat, half cabin configuration, operated by one person. His chief responsibility on the night was to protect the fireworks barges, moored at intervals along the river's east, and ensure that nonauthorised boats remained well clear. The boat's radios fitted in front of the passenger seat, its volume turned up due to the loud music being pumped out by large public address speakers set out along the river. This presented a problem, as I would likely find it difficult to hear MAS controllers via my portable radio. The only option that seemed viable to overcome this was for me to position myself behind the driver's seat, as far away from his radio as possible. I held onto the back of his seat with one hand, the other holding my portable radio. And so it was, from about nine o'clock, we patrolled up and down our section of river at less than walking speed, without a case.

The crowds had built up dramatically, particularly along the river banks. I wondered how I would get through to a patient should I be called. Prior to midnight, I attended only one patient, a young man who had fallen from a barge into the river. Other than being cold, he was unharmed. As midnight approached, we were near Swan Street bridge, when from beneath it a pleasure craft appeared, packed with party-makers, heading for one of the fireworks barges. My "captain" spotted them and reacted by immediately swinging his wheel to the right, at the same time giving the engine full throttle and causing the boat's bow to rise steeply. I lost my grip on his seat and was flung backwards, landing heavily on top of my equipment, which I'd stored in the boat's open rear. Despite it being summer, it was a cold night, and I was wearing my reasonably padded ambulance jacket. I felt sharp pains, especially in my right shoulder. Realising what had happened, my captain brought the boat to a stop and apologetically helped me to my feet. Despite the intense pain, I didn't believe I had suffered any fractures, only bruising. I decided to carry on with the shift, although before I could reconsider, I received a call to come to Doug's assistance at a possible cardiac arrest case, near the mooring location of the restored sailing ship, the *Polly Woodside.*

We motored downriver, but as we approached the *Polly Woodside,* I found that there was no easy access from the water level to the quayside, several metres above me. I decided to climb the horizontal beams along the river edge and then ask the captain to pass up my gear. I did this, noting my increasing shoulder pain. I'd no sooner reached the top only to receive a cancellation—the case was not a cardiac arrest.

As midnight had come and gone, it was clear to all, including MAS, that the Millennium Bug was much ado about very little at all. By 3 a.m., ambulance cases along the river seemed to have dried up (pun intended), and crowds had dispersed. By this time, my pain was such that I advised MAS controllers that I was going off shift. Prior to this, though, my captain provided some entertainment. He told me that he wanted to pick up some food, and so he tied the boat off along the river bank. I told him I would wait, as I couldn't leave my equipment. He had just left when I noticed that the rope he had attached was unravelling from where he had tied it off. I had to scramble along the boat's length and reattach it; otherwise, the boat and I would have drifted off down the river. When he returned, I asked him to take me to either police boat and drop me off.

I arrived home but was unable to sleep due to the pain. Belen took me to hospital, where X-rays didn't reveal any fractures. It was recommended that I attend a series of physiotherapist sessions aimed at decreasing my level of pain, which remained undiminished. This I did for the next few months; in the end, it only exacerbated my pain. Finally, in May 2000, an MRI was done, which showed that I had suffered a shoulder fracture at the glenoid labrum, an injury not usually identified by X-ray alone. The physiotherapy sessions, though well-intended, had resulted in further damage. Following this diagnosis, my right shoulder was reconstructed, although after I recovered, I experienced right arm paresthesia. I was recommended a variety of treatments, both to reduce ongoing pain and to relieve the parasthesia. One of the more unusual treatments was one first tried on World War I soldiers who were suffering pain due to restricted shoulder and neck movement whilst serving in trenches during winters. The treatment involves insertion of long, thin scalpel blades into both sides of the neck, sweeping these backwards and forwards, thereby severing and releasing some of the muscle fibres. This done, the patient should experience increased mobility and pain reduction. My treatment was conducted in the surgeon's consulting room. I was seated upright, and the surgeon began by injecting local anaesthesia. After waiting a few minutes for this to take effect, he inserted the scalpel, and I felt it enter the muscle above my shoulder, just to the left of my neck. The pain was intense, and I suddenly felt faint and fell from the chair. My blood pressure had plummeted, but after laying flat for a period, I recovered. The surgeon asked if I wished him to continue; I declined. Fortunately, Belen was with me and drove me home.

To discover the cause of my ongoing parathesia, I was again scanned, resulting in a finding of severe cervical disc damage and dangerous narrowing of space at the spinal nerve roots. Further surgery was necessary, resulting in the removal of two discs, which were replaced by carbon fibre discs, followed by fusion using bone grafted from my hip. The story of my injuries and ongoing issues continues. Further surgery and fusion has been offered, but I declined. I relate this life-changing event, as it illustrates the sometimes unexpected outcome of paramedic work (granted that in this case, the circumstances were unusual).

20

I Have What?

By 1986, I had seven years of operational experience as an AO and two years as a MICA officer. I was thirty-four, and despite feeling a general fatigue due to shift work, I felt fine. Regular periods of leave helped, but most of us found that it was not until the third week of a four-week break that we began to feel well, having regained some of our energy.

It was during a routine four-week break that I became ill. I was caring at home for our son, Julian, who was about eighteen months old. Belen was at work, teaching English as a second language. Without any warning, I felt suddenly unwell, but without any real physical symptoms. I was fairly certain though that I shouldn't ignore how I felt. I picked Julian up and took him to his local creche, then drove the short distance to our GP's surgery. The receptionist must have noticed something in me, as my usual GP appeared and took me into her room. I tried to describe what was happening but just burst into tears and couldn't seem to stop. She took me into another room equipped with a bed, and I think I fell asleep. At some point, she returned, telling me that I had to go to the Melbourne Clinic in Richmond, without delay.

I wasn't familiar with the clinic or its services. My next recollections are fragmented. I know that I drove myself but found that I fell asleep at each red light, only to be startled awake by irate drivers honking their horns. I don't recall arriving at the clinic, but I was shown to a private room. I was totally bewildered, feeling ill as I'd never experienced before in my life. Belen arrived and brought me some clothes and other things, but the rest of her visit is a blank. Next I recall having to queue up with other patients to receive my medication from a nurse through a small window. I took these as instructed but soon after felt even more confused and ill. I think the medications included Stelazine and lithium, I'm not sure.

A patient approached me during a mealtime. She turned out to be Belen's former teaching colleague. Disturbingly, she told me that she and all the other patients had previously been admitted to the clinic. Was this to be my future? At this stage, it was slowly dawning on me that I was in a mental health facility. For the first few days, I was still waiting to see a doctor. Belen complained to the staff.

Finally, I met my assigned psychiatrist and questioned in my mind why I needed to see him. Belen was with me, and she asked him the questions that wouldn't come to my mind. He explained, "You are suffering a decompensation crisis, and you have obsessive compulsive disorder (OCD)." He explained how he had arrived at his finding, adding that decompensation crisis replaced the former term of nervous breakdown. I had never heard of OCD, so he also explained its common features. I seem to recall that I thought he didn't know what he was talking about. I thought back and other than growing up as a "worrier," I couldn't relate to the OCD behaviours that he outlined. Belen raised her concerns regarding the side effects of the drugs I'd been prescribed. I think changes were made, but again I'm not sure. I was returned to the clinic and asked if I wished to join a group therapy discussion. I remained convinced that I didn't need to be at the clinic and had nothing to discuss, so I declined. My parents arrived from Geelong, but I don't think they understood why I was there. It wasn't until many years later that I realised what Belen had been through and what a wonderful, strong, and loving advocate she had been. She somehow continued to work during this time whilst caring for both Julian and his fifteen-year-old sister, Shirley.

I remained an inpatient, and one day, during Belen's visit, we were advised that I should receive electroconvulsive therapy (ECT). Belen told me much later that she strongly argued against this; she definitely did not want this for me. Despite her layperson's medical knowledge, she was confident of her instincts and stuck by them. I know she was right. I didn't receive ECT; instead, various medication regimes were tried, none of which contributed to my becoming well. Again, I can't be sure, but I think I was at the clinic for about two weeks. Neither am I sure of the circumstances regarding how I left the clinic, whether I was discharged or Belen just decided to take me home. I know that she was never confident that the clinic or the drugs were leading to any improvement. I wish I could tell her now, but I'm sure she would have made a great paramedic.

Being back at home felt very peculiar; nothing seemed familiar, and for some reason, I found that I couldn't go near our garage. I don't know when it first occurred, but I found myself checking and rechecking light switches and door locks. I had no choice now but to accept the psychiatrist's diagnosis of OCD.

I could not have been home long, as my leave period came to an end, and I decided to return to my regular MICA roster. In hindsight, this was a very poor decision. I did not tell colleagues or managers of my time in the clinic or my diagnoses. Times were different, and I must have feared for my future employment and the stigma of mental illness should I reveal what had happened. The first two patients we attended, I was convinced, were suffering from decompensation crises; I'm sure they came to no harm, as my colleague would have intervened.

I tried to conceal my OCD habits and behaviour from my colleagues. If anyone had noticed anything unusual, no one commented, at least to my face. I was not concerned that my OCD would impact adversely on my patients; if anything, the checking and rechecking of drugs we were about to administer probably reduced the chance of an error being made.

OCD, at least in my experience, had the effect of completely stripping away all of my self-confidence and, in some sense, who I was. Simple actions and everyday activities that previously I would not have given a second thought became difficult and frustrating. I felt an unrelenting compulsion to repeat tasks, checking a heater was turned off or a car door was locked. I added to the list of tasks as time went on. OCD causes feelings of guilt for an endless array of imagined scenarios. I found when driving to or from a shift that I imagined that I might have caused an accident. I returned to where I thought it might have happened, sometimes again and again. Anger, fatigue, and frustration took over, as intellectually I knew that nothing had happened, but I could not stop until I had somehow convinced myself that all was well. Maddening and mad, at the same time.

My beautiful and long-suffering wife always knew that if I was late coming home and not on a late case, I was probably indulging my OCD. She would call me, understandably become angry with me, and sometimes this was enough for me to stop and drive home. The knowledge that the condition (mental illness or however one chooses to define it) is relatively common provides little comfort. I was interested to read that many medical staff are OCD afflicted and over-represented, relative to the general population.

Over the past few years, Belen frequently told me how proud she was of my recovery efforts. I always reminded her, though, that it was through her love and support that I was able to make any progress at all. Today, I am not free of OCD; her death caused it to come out of its relative hibernation. Because of Belen, I will strive to keep it under control; she deserves nothing less. I have only been able to write about my illnesses as I feel I must honour Belen and all that she has done for me.

21

Belen

I have dedicated this book to my wife, Belen, a small tribute to a magnificent, shining soul. I present the reader with the following brief synopsis of her life, certainly well lived. Belen achieved her Bachelor of Science Degree in Elementary Education in the Philippines in 1967. Having immigrated to Australia with her (our) daughter, Shirley in 1973, she taught in primary and secondary education for a number of years. Always seeking to further her own education, she was awarded a Diploma of Teaching (Primary) from Victoria College in 1988. Reflecting on her experiences as a migrant, she decided to focus her later career on teaching English as a second language (ESL). In 1991, she received a Graduate Diploma of Education (Teaching English to Speakers of Other Languages) from the University of South Australia.

From 1991 through to her retirement in 2012, she taught ESL to migrant students arriving from Africa, Europe, Asia, and South America (she spoke Spanish fluently). During these years, she received many accolades from her students and teaching colleagues. Her efforts to assist her students were not limited to teaching ESL. She actively sought job placements for many of them, visited them on site, and was often rewarded by her students being given full- or part-time employment.

In her final teaching years at the Chisholm Institute at Frankston, her job began to demand much more of her than her teaching duties.

Working in isolation from the main Chisholm Institute in Dandenong, she gradually took on all the related administrative tasks, unsupported. The volume of work whilst also coping with the institute's internal wranglings left her stressed and exhausted. I asked her on may occasions to consider retiring, but this remained something she wanted to do when the time was right for her.

Finally though, enough was too much, and she resigned in August 2012. Not long after her retirement, she suffered an episode of bradycardia and hypotension. It quickly resolved, but soon after this, she began having brief episodes of atrial fibrillation (AF). Her GP at the time was dismissive, attributing her AF to the aging process. I remonstrated with the GP, reminding him that no patient should have his or her symptoms so easily dismissed, and that in Belen's case, she had never been seriously unwell in her life. An apology was received, but Belen had lost confidence in the GP and the practice in general. Despite the additional travel time, she elected to return to her former GP for her future care.

This GP referred her to a cardiologist, Dr Logan Bittinger. As her AF episodes were increasing in frequency, he prescribed her appropriate medication, including Warfarin. This resulted in decreasing the frequency of her episodes, although she required weekly blood tests to monitor her Warfarin levels. She was always anxious prior to each blood test, fearing and detesting the needle. She bravely persisted; however, her AF episodes continued. I asked her to always advise me when she was symptomatic, usually reflected by central chest tightness and fatigue. At times, though, she didn't want me to know, although a quick check of her pulse confirmed yet another episode.

Never having been seriously ill, taking medication was an anathema to Belen. Dr Bittinger, who over a period of time had also become our friend, advised that should medication fail to resolve her recurring AF episodes, cardiac ablation was likely to be a better long-term solution and should also result in her eventually being free of medication. Briefly, cardiac ablation is a routine, low-risk procedure, whereby a catheter is inserted via an incision in the thigh then directed into the heart. Tests then pinpoint the area suspected to be the source of AF, which is then either frozen or cauterized, preventing further AF outbreaks. Belen considered this option for some time, though she persisted with her medication regime. As her father had passed away in hospital at a relatively young age, she was reluctant to undergo the ablation procedure.

Her AF episodes continued in frequency and duration into September 2013. Belen was always full of life and radiated love and happiness, and she was always stylishly dressed. Despite her AF, she continued to love and care for Shirley, Julian, and me, unconditionally. She doted on Shirley and her husband Alistair's children, Darcy and Patrick, leaving them never in doubt that they were loved. She continued to work on her pride, her garden, although she was annoyed by me offering her frequent cups of tea, but really hoping that she would just take a break.

Many times, we discussed if we should pursue the cardiac ablation option, with its promise of a future free from AF and medication. The final decision, though, had to be hers; I would support her whatever she decided. She wanted to better understand what the procedure entailed, so we returned to see Dr Bittinger, with Belen's list of questions in hand. He explained that the risks of complications were low and there was an 80 percent chance or greater that the procedure would successfully eliminate her AF. In the event that the procedure failed, it could be repeated at a later date. By the end of the consultation, Belen had made up her mind to go ahead. Her procedure was booked at the Valley Private Hospital for October 13, 2014.

On the morning of October 12, Belen asked if we could visit St Francis Church in Lonsdale Street to light some candles in memory of her father, to whom she had been close. She often honoured him in this way, always in the same St Francis chapel. Having done this, we decided to have lunch in the city, then as her procedure coincided with my sister-in-law, Jean's, birthday, we decided to visit her and my brother Aafko on the way home. Jean, a theatre nurse, asked Belen if she was at all nervous about the pending procedure.

She replied, "I'm not worried, I have my MICA man with me."

Belen's own photo showing a portion of her garden, taken in spring 2013, shortly before her passing.

As always, Belen dressed beautifully on the morning of her procedure. Our son, Julian, saw her off at our front door; he was comforted by her beaming smile as we left. Our daughter, Shirley, and family had left for a break in Fiji on the same day. Belen did not want her to worry and was keen to surprise her on her return with an improved health outlook.

Belen was admitted into the Valley Hospital Coronary Care Unit (CCU) and retired to bed to await her procedure. She was anxious but remained in good spirits. As she was wheeled to the catheter lab, she asked me, "Will you be here when I come back?" I thought her question a little odd, as she knew I would not move until she returned. Perhaps minutes later, Dr Bittinger appeared and advised me that the procedure had been successful and provided instructions regarding Belen's medication for the forthcoming weeks. I felt much relieved and returned to my book, waiting for her return to the CCU, where she would need to be monitored overnight.

A short time later, Dr Bittinger returned, appearing pale and distressed. He asked me to follow him to a private room. My mind and body tensed in fear. We sat down and he said, "We can't wake her up. We think she's had a bleed." At that moment, and without having seen her, I knew she was lost. I felt completely helpless; all my years of ambulance experience were of no use. I could do nothing to help my wife and best friend. A neurosurgeon was urgently despatched from St Vincent's Private Hospital to relieve Belen's intra-cranial pressure; once this was done, I was able to see her. I took her hand and looked into her eyes, seeing as I had in so many patients that her spirit had departed.

An ambulance arrived to transfer her to St Vincent's, and I asked the crew, one of whom I knew, if I could care for Belen on the way. The neurosureon climbed in the back, and I sat behind Belen's bandaged head, She remained intubated and nonbreathing; I ventilated her via the all-too-familiar black rubber bag through to our arrival at about 8 p.m.

I sat with her through the night, her condition unchanged. Shirley had been contacted and flew back from Fiji alone, unaware of Belen's grave condition. I spoke with the ICU director and asked him pointedly if in his opinion Belen had any chance of recovery. It was a rhetorical question, to which he replied, "No." I asked if we could review her MRI scans taken at the Valley Private. These showed very extensive sub-arachnoid bleeding throughout her brain.

The following day, Belen's blood pressure became erratic; her AF had returned. Her spirit had departed, but her body struggled on. I was asked about organ donation, not a topic we had ever discussed between us. I was anxious, though, that she be returned to me as intact as possible; her body had endured enough trauma, and so I declined the request.

Two days after her ICU admission, her body was beginning to fail, requiring drugs to maintain her BP. I spoke again with the ICU director, telling him that I thought her body had suffered enough. Shirley and I returned to Belen's bedside, prayed, and waited as all life support was withdrawn. Julian was unable to cope with seeing his mother this way. Belen's physical struggle was over.

I understood that as her passing had been unexpected, the coroner would require an autopsy to determine cause of death. I knew what this meant and again wanted my beautiful wife returned to me intact. The ICU director was empathetic and spoke with the coroner's office, who agreed that an autopsy was not necessary.

The following days were a blur of activity, grief, and confusion. I could not and would not accept that Belen was not coming home; nevertheless, her funeral and service had to be arranged. I chose the songs that I knew she would love, while Shirley and Alistair compiled a beautiful accompanying photographic memorial. Over our years together, Belen would sometimes joke that if she passed away, I had to apply her makeup. I always responded angrily as the thought of life without her was something I could not contemplate. Together, Shirley and I applied her makeup as best we could; with or without, she remained beautiful.

My life ended with Belen's, taken over by an existence where I tried to carry on, always mindful of what she would have wanted for me. I have no self-pity, only an enduring sadness for Belen, that she did not live to enjoy our retirement and participate in the lives of our children and grandchildren.

We had planned to return to Europe in 2015. Instead, I travelled alone, revisiting some of our favourite places. As she had done for her father, I lit candles for her at cathedrals and churches we had previously visited together. I photographed them and incorporated them into a book I wrote for our family, dedicated to her memory.

If the reading of this book has been of any value, it is because of Belen. Tragically, Belen did not meet Julian's daughter Zoe, who was born only days after her passing.

Candles lit for Belen at Notre Dame Cathedral, Paris

I realised during the course of my writing that there was a gap. I needed to know how she faced her ablation procedure once she was wheeled away from me. I contacted Dr Bittinger and explained my need, and he had no hesitation in agreeing to meet me for a coffee.

Belen and I had become familiar with Dr Bittinger, who we both found to be genuinely caring, supportive, and patient. He was clearly shocked and disturbed when Belen could not be awakened from anaesthesia. He honoured her memory by attending her funeral. I thanked him for his care and expressed my belief that her haemorrhage could not have been anticipated.

I met Logan at a Brighton café in July 2016. He told me that despite Belen being nervous and anxious, she approched her pending procedure with courage. He had taken her hand and once again explained the procedure., then left her in the hands of the anaesthetist.

Logan reminded me that each time we visited him, Belen's lively personality always shone through. He remembered her fashion sense and her amazing array of jewellery. He keeps her funeral memorial card in his desk drawer both as a reminder of her and also as a prompt to ensure that he always gets to know and understand his patients and their needs and fears. For him, this is her legacy. Before parting, I again thanked him for his care for both Belen and me and told him that he always enjoyed our trust and confidence.

22

Reflections

The cases I've described in this book reflect only a small slice of my twenty-three years of operational ambulance service, shared with many colleagues. Despite the passing of fifteen years when my operational career ended, the mental images of each case are sharp, as are many others I've not included. The workings of human memory can be perplexing. Perhaps it is not surprising that as paramedics, we recall cases that were particularly traumatic or from which we learned valuable lessons. David Cooper visited me as I was competing the final draft of this book. I mentioned that he and I were crewed together at several of the cases I've described. David commented that he was sure that I'd described a particular case where again we were crewed together. He told me that we had been despatched to Rosebud Hospital to transfer a critically ill patient to Frankston Hospital. The patient had suffered extensive head and facial injuries when he was struck by a vehicle's mirror as he was crossing the road. Rosebud Hospital was not equipped to manage time-critical patients, and on our arrival, his treating doctor advised us that he didn't expect the patient to survive the journey.

I was jockey but only vaguely recall having difficulty managing the patient's airway due to his gross facial injuries. As we came down Oliver's Hill, leading into Frankston, the patient expired. David told me that I became very angry and told him, "When I started in ambulance, I promised myself that no one would die in the back of my ambulance."

169

What disturbed me when David related my comment and my reaction was my naivety in making such a promise, one that I could never fulfill. Perhaps my reaction was due to my youth, or perhaps I was already exhibiting signs of stress. Whatever the case, it appears that I had blocked out this experience; if David had not related it to me, I would not have been able to recall the first time a patient had died during transport.

I retired from AV in 2013 but remain in regular contact with many of my former operational and nonoperational colleagues, many of whom are dear friends. After sharing the work and humour over the years, what remains is a strong bond, binding us together.

In January 2016, I travelled alone to Normandy in northern France, a country whose culture, language, and music I love. I rented a small *gite* just outside the village of St Marie du Mont, where I could work on my book draft, undisturbed. I chose this area also as I have long had a strong interest in World War II history. One of the main D-Day landing beaches was only a few minutes' drive away. Being January, it was certainly cold, but this meant that many of the WWII sites surrounding this part of Normandy were free from other tourists. This was how I found Omaha Beach, made famous again by the movie *Saving Private Ryan*. I walked the length of the deserted beach, trying to imagine the horrific D-Day scenes. Sacrifice was the term that kept coming to mind.

Some of my former paramedic colleagues have indeed sacrificed themselves, just as tragically and unnecessarily as many of the troops that came ashore on Omaha Beach.

I have no sense of regret for choosing ambulance as a career. I remain proud of my achievements throughout my career, although I've learned to appreciate that this pride came with the cost of sometimes neglecting my role as a husband and father. I would not and could not admit it, particularly during my operational years, that I had allowed ambulance to dominate my life. This was a mistake. Having confessed this, other paramedics will understand that being a paramedic is far more than just a job; for many, it is a vocation, one that becomes an inherent part of us.

Finally, I would like to remind current and future paramedics that as much as it is important to save the lives of strangers, this also applies to you. Having chosen this unique profession, you owe it to yourself, your partner, and your families to take care of your own health and wellbeing. Thank you for reading my story.

Folllowing Belen's passing, I returned to France in 2015. I needed time to be alone and to think about how I would write a book about her. I stayed in Uzes, a small market village in Provence. I walked every day, finding paths that I doubted were frequented by tourists. One hot day, I was walking such a path outside the village when I looked down to see a rock painted with the description shown in the photograph below. I wondered about its origin, why it was in English, and whether I was meant to come across it. I share it with you.

Printed in the United States
By Bookmasters